Adoption Means Love:
Triumph of the Heart

ADOPTION

TRIBE™

PUBLISHING

An Adoption Tribe Hard Cover
Published by
Adoption Tribe Publishing
211 W. San Francisco Street
Suite 201
Santa Fe, NM 87501

Library of Congress Cataloging in
Publication Data
Madrid-Branch, Michelle
Adoption Means Love: Triumph
of the Heart
Michelle Madrid-Branch
p.   cm.
Includes footnote references

ISBN 0-9747443-1-X
1. Adoption.
2. Adopted children.
3. Adoptees.
I. Title.

Book Design
Tom Morin & Isabella Gonzales
Context Design Inc.
Galisteo, New Mexico
www.contextdesign.com

Printing and Binding
Karen Powelson
CS Graphics, (Singapore)
Santa Fe, New Mexico

Primary Photography
Cathy Maier Callanan
Cathy Maier Callanan Photography,
Santa Fe, New Mexico
www.cmcphoto.com

Editors
Kim Berrian
Michelle Madrid-Branch
Laura O'Bagy

Dedication

This book is dedicated to my husband, Jeffrey:
may we continue to cling to our triple-braided cord.

To my son, Christian Alexander: *I marvel at the
miracle of you, sweet boy.*

And, to the millions of children around the world
who wait for their forever families...*there is hope.*

Adoption Means Love...

Contents

Acknowledgements

Michelle Madrid-Branch wishes to thank each story contributor within the pages of **Adoption Means Love: Triumph of the Heart.** *We are stronger when we share our stories!* She would like to thank Kim Berrian, author of *Natural Wealth,* for his partnership in this project. *I could not have done it without you, Kim.* To Marshall Thurber, who is my mentor and friend, *my gratitude is eternal.* And finally, to my husband, Jeffrey, whose support is angelic. *I am forever blessed to have you in my life.*

Above all, my gratitude to God — thank you for the lesson taught in 1 Corinthians 13:13. *Three things will endure: faith, hope, and love. But the greatest of these is love.*

Additional thanks to the National Council For Adoption, for its continued support and guidance.

Preface

Dear Friend of Adoption,

The words you are about to read are real stories from real people. These adoption accounts will take you around the globe, weaving a common thread of transformation and triumph.

Powerfully, each story contributor highlights the truth behind the miracle of family formation called adoption. It has been my pleasure and honor to travel this journey with each contributor. Their personal adoption moments have warmed my heart and deepened my resolve to share the *Adoption Means Love* message with the world.

It is now my pleasure and honor to share this experience with you.

—*Michelle Madrid-Branch*

I

"It is my fondest hope that all children in waiting will discover a beautiful adoption heritage and their place in this Adoption Tribe."
—*Michelle Madrid-Branch*

Capt. Thomas Coram,
1668-1751
Portrait by William
Hogarth (1740)
By kind permission of
Coram Family in the care of
the Foundling Museum.

Carrying the Torch

I am a firm believer in honoring both biological heritage and adoption heritage. As a person of adoption, I see both as precious fabrics sewn into my 'quilt of life.' I'd like to share a bit of my personal family ancestry, as we begin turning the pages of ***Triumph of the Heart.***

My adoption heritage links me to a very important person who was, as I call him, a Founding Father in my Adoption Tribe. Thomas Coram was born in England, the country of my birth, in the year 1668. His hometown was that of Lyme Regis, one of the loveliest and oldest of English seaports. Thomas' father is believed to have been a master mariner. Thomas, himself, spent much of his early life at sea. In fact, it is documented that he first went to sea at eleven years of age.

In 1694, Coram landed in Taunton, Massachusetts. He operated a ship building business until 1703 when he returned to England. Upon his return, he became a successful merchant in London and began promoting trade with the American colonies, particularly with the colony of Georgia, which was rich in pine trees for tar. For the next 16 years he found himself taking cargoes to and from America. During this time, he grew keenly aware of the needs and possibilities of colonial enterprise. In 1732, Thomas Coram became a trustee of James Oglethorpe's Georgia colony, which was named after King George II.

Later in his life, Thomas Coram the 'sailor and builder of empires' became Thomas Coram the 'philanthropist'. Appalled by the spread of abandoned and homeless children found on the streets of London, he obtained in the year 1739 a Royal Charter granted by King George II. The charter established a hospital for the safekeeping and education of deserted children. The Thomas Coram Foundling Hospital was completed in 1740 and became the world's first incorporated charity.

Thomas Coram died in 1751, yet his name lives on today in the *Coram Family Adoption and Permanent Families Service,* one of the United Kingdom's leading adoption agencies. The Thomas Coram Research Unit, another way in which Coram's legacy lives on, is a multidisciplinary research unit focusing on children both inside and outside of their family unit.

My adoptive mother's tie to Thomas Coram is through his younger brother, William, who set sail to America and then traveled to Georgia. My mother is linked to William's lineage. Her maiden name is Coram from Thomasville, Georgia. Thomas Coram is her Great-Great-Great-Great Uncle.

Through adoption, Thomas Coram is my Great-Great-Great-Great-Great Uncle. However, I feel as if he is also one of my guardian angels. We were both born in England and drawn to America. Georgia became an important symbol for us both: it is where Coram left his fingerprint on America and it is the birthplace of my adoptive parents who have left their fingerprints on my heart.

In a book entitled, *Thomas Coram,* by H.F.B. Compston, it is written: *"He said what he meant, and meant what he said. Men believed in him. His unselfishness was conspicuous: he spent and was spent for the good causes he had at heart. He loved his Church, he loved his country, he loved little children."*

I feel an essence of Coram's spirit within me as I reach out to the world and share a message of triumph through adoption. He cared for discarded British children even when it seemed that the rest of his countrymen did not. He cared for me, I feel, long before this British girl was even born.

Thomas Coram and I do not share a biological kinship. We do, however, share a spiritual one. I am proud to claim this beautiful adoption heritage. I am honored to take my place in this Adoption Tribe.

We must carry the torch. **We must all carry the torch.**

—*Michelle Madrid-Branch,* New Mexico

---

[1]H.F.B. Compston, *Thomas Coram: Churchman, Empire Builder, and Philanthropist* (London: Society for Promoting Christian Knowledge, 1918), 139

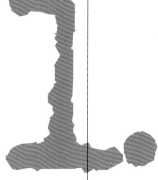

Remembering the Love of Life-Givers

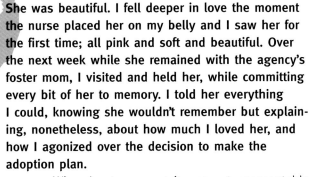

She Was Beautiful

She was beautiful. I fell deeper in love the moment the nurse placed her on my belly and I saw her for the first time; all pink and soft and beautiful. Over the next week while she remained with the agency's foster mom, I visited and held her, while committing every bit of her to memory. I told her everything I could, knowing she wouldn't remember but explaining, nonetheless, about how much I loved her, and how I agonized over the decision to make the adoption plan.

When I got pregnant it was not unacceptable for a woman to have a child out of wedlock. It was, however, during a time when adoption seemed to be relatively unheard of and even viewed negatively by some. I chose adoption regardless, not out of shame or fear, but out of love; a deep kenotic love that realizes love of other over love of self.

I experienced such profound beauty over the nine months that I carried her. I knew those months were all we would have together, so I savored every moment and created an intimate world for the two of us. I would talk to her all day long, telling her what we were doing, where we were going, and who we were seeing. I cherished the movements and kicks, the tiny hiccups and rapid heartbeat. I cried joyfully when I saw her first ultrasound and I named her when the tech told me she was a girl. I wanted to keep her there, in my womb, safe from the world and with me forever.

And all the while, I was researching and learning about adoption, weighing my options as to what would be in her best interest. I had to consider what I wanted for her: a family, stability, a chance for a good future. My situation at that time would have been a terrible burden on her. I had to be realistic about my limitations because the risk was so great. I found an agency and began working with the social worker. She was a lovely woman, supportive and genuine and not once did she pressure me. I prayed to make the right decision and in my gut I knew the answer. It was about her. It had to be. Even though I felt so strongly convicted to my decision, it did not make it any less painful.

I felt moments of deep loneliness, sadness, and even anger. I had never encountered feelings so deep before or since. While some close family members and friends were supportive, others made careless and callous comments. So I remained cloistered at a friend's house for much of the nine months to avoid further criticism while at times feeling acutely alone and isolated. Then came the day when the social worker brought me five family profiles from which to choose. After reading the profiles, I forcefully threw them across the room, rejecting each and every one of them. My anger was in control and my initial reaction was that none of these families would raise my daughter. Once the emotions subsided, one family seemed to emerge from the now scattered pile. I did not feel that they were better than me. I felt that they were in a better situation than me. At my request, the social worker arranged a meeting with them soon after the choice was made. Despite the desperate blinding tears on the way to the agency, upon meeting them, I felt tremendous peace. It is this family I chose for her, and the one she has today.

As my delivery date came closer, the pain and sadness intensified. I knew what I was doing and why I was doing it, yet this knowledge did not take away the sense of loss that I was feeling — the loss of her and the loss of being her parent. It was that rip-out-your-heart kind of pain — the kind that physically hurts. As I prepared for the day when I would say goodbye, I began therapy and worked on strategies that would help get me through the days and months of grief that would inevitably follow the delivery. I prepared as best I could, knowing that nothing could stop the onslaught of emotions.

And there she was, on my belly; all pink and soft and beautiful. While I fell deeper in love with her in that moment, I also knew love sometimes requires sacrifice. My heart was heavy and a storm of emotions swirled around me; however, I knew my decision for adoption was a good one and it was right. I also knew that once she went to her family, I had to let go of her completely. So at the agency's foster mom's house, I mothered her and cherished her...and then I let her go.

Although I could not present her to her family, I did meet with them briefly, moments before she arrived at the agency. I congratulated them on their new daughter. And then with a hollow ache deep in my heart and a horrible emptiness in my arms, I left. There are no words to describe the grief that followed. In a way it was like a death, yet very different; it wasn't death at all. The days and months that followed all blurred together in waves of tears and sadness, yet in the midst of it all, there remained a sense of peace. I knew that the pain would not last forever and as the grief slowly subsided, I began to feel the beauty of what had taken place. This was not death. This was life. A family had been created out of love.

It's been over a decade now and I continue to think of her; however, there is no grief or longing anymore as I no longer feel emptiness or hollowness. She taught me things about myself that I never imagined before and has transformed my life in a powerful way. Most importantly, she taught me how to love in the purest sense — with the good of the other as the only purpose. And I bring that lesson with me as I move forward in life. Although I gave the joy of raising her to another, she is with me always; all pink and soft and beautiful.

—*Anonymous Author*

Phyllis and I decided to wait a couple of years after our marriage to start a family. We wanted to enjoy married life – just the two of us – before expanding. Our perfect plan didn't seem so perfect, though, when the desire to have children arrived but our advanced ages suggested we would have no luck in this regard.

We considered the use of fertility drugs but felt that the uncertainty of the results did not justify the costly investment. Then, Phyllis and I realized there was a much more viable option available: adoption.

Our first formal steps toward adoption began in November of 1996. We were excited to finally start the qualification process that would, hopefully, lead to parenthood. In July of 1997, we became certified to enter the pool of prospective adoptive parents. Understanding that the average wait was at least two years, we remained cautiously optimistic that our profiles would be chosen.

Imagine my shock, when just two months later, I received a call at work from our caseworker. She advised me that a birthmother, who was well into her pregnancy, had tentatively chosen us as adoptive parents for her baby. Thrilled and amazed, I could barely think of a single thing to say and, in a state of pure numbness, I thanked her for the phone call and hung up. I waited to share the news with Phyllis until I arrived home that evening. Shaking from excitement and nearly in tears, I sat my wife on my lap and said, "We've been chosen as prospective adoptive parents!"

The whirlwind of activity began...
We readied a nursery, met with the birth families, and prayed that we were meeting their expectations. On two occasions, the birthmother's parents interviewed us. Their role was to ensure that Phyllis and I were the proper choice to raise their daughter's

baby. This was a particularly critical aspect of the selection process, since the birthmother planned on the kind of "open adoption"* where an on-going relationship between adoptive parents and birth families is carried out.

Christopher was born in the early morning hours of December 12, 1997. We rushed to the hospital to meet the baby who would, soon, be the absolute center of our life. The first call I made was to my mother who had all along been enamored and excited over our decision to adopt. She told me, "I'm going by the hospital tonight so I can have a glimpse of Christopher through one of those nursery windows."

As it turned out, my mom couldn't find Christopher in the nursery and proceeded to locate the birthmother's room where she knocked on the door, met the birthmother, and spent several hours holding and feeding Christopher. The birth family was extremely happy to see how excited his adoptive grand-mother was to meet him!

Eight months later, we understood the motivation behind my mom's visit that night. In August of 1998, Mom emotionally and tearfully broke the news that she had arranged an adoption plan for a baby boy she gave birth to nearly forty-three years earlier. She continued to explain that her son, Dan, had recently located her and they had made plans to meet.

I also learned that Dan's birthday was December 13th, one day after Christopher's birth date. We thank God that Dan found Mom when he did and that they had nearly one and a half years together before her sudden death on December 12th, 1999, Christopher's second birthday.

Although Mom left us far too soon, we are comforted by the fact that she had the opportunity to establish a heartwarming relationship with Dan. Indeed, this is our tale of two adoptions; how powerful is the bond!

—*Mark Haas,* Virginia
*A definition of Open Adoption can be found in the Glossary of Terms.

The Greatest Joy

Nicolette, Matthew, Corina and Thomas

I have adopted four children internationally, two girls and one boy, from the country of Romania. Our fourth child, a toddler boy, we adopted from Guatemala. It has long been my dream to find their birth families and to introduce our children to them.

In 1991, when we adopted Nicolette and Matthew from Romania, I requested pictures of their birth families. During the court session, I was honored to meet both Nic and Matt's birthmothers. Although we were only able to visit for five minutes, I filled that time with my heartfelt gratitude to be given such beautiful children to raise. I added that I would do everything in my power to be the very best mom. During that short visit, I also videotaped my children's birthmothers and took photos that I included in a very special memory album.

At the age of seven, my children began to ask questions about adoption and during many nighttime conversations I would remind them that the saddest day of their birthmothers' lives was the happiest day of mine. Unable to answer the question of 'why' their adoptions occurred, I would simply say that Romania is a poor country with little opportunity.

In 1997 we adopted our third child, Corina, from Romania as well. Once again, I asked for photos of the birth family and was disappointed to hear that the lawyer had none to give. I took action and hired a driver to take me to the home of my little girl's birth family. Upon meeting the birth family, I found that they were kind, warm and beautiful people. I felt sad to learn how very poor they were and told them how we would take the very best care of Corina. I took many pictures and documented family history, which truly has been a positive thing.

Over the years, Corina has sent and received pictures and letters from her birth family and that contact has meant the world to her. For Nic and Matt, however, there was no contact with their birth families as locating them had proven difficult. My promise was that one day we would go back to Romania and find them.

That day came in July of 2003, as we boarded a plane for Bucharest and headed to my children's native land to uncover their history. We hoped to locate all three birth families of my Romanian children. This was our prayer and the one thing we focused on.

We began with Nicolette's family. With the assistance of a local police station, we were led to the area where our daughter's birth family lives. As we drove through the village, we were shocked and saddened by the poverty all around us. Most of the children, playing on the streets, were without clothes and shoes.

Pulling up to the home, I immediately recognized Nic's birthmother (even after twelve years) and jumped out of the van to meet her. I began showing pictures of Nicolette to her birthmother and she started crying and kissing each photo exclaiming how happy she was to know that Nic was alive and well. When Nicolette got out of the van, her birthmother would not let go of her and held her hand for the rest of the visit. We learned that Nic had two brothers and two sisters, one of which had been adopted by a family in Belgium. Nicolette was truly happy to see the degree at which her birth family cared for her.

The next morning, we were back in our van as we set out for a four-hour drive to the town where we hoped to find Matthew's birth family. Matt was nervous and Nicolette was still floating on cloud nine. Corina, meanwhile was observing everyone in the van and our son Thomas, from Guatemala, was being an angel in his car seat.

Once again, we stopped at the local police station and asked for assistance. The police officers were extremely helpful, adding that Matt's birth family had lived in this village for years. They offered to show us the way and the Mayor extended his hand and offered to accommodate us with anything we needed.

The main street of the town was pretty and lined with flowers, but once we entered the village we were met with serious poverty. I recognized Matt's birthmother and got out of our van to show her pictures of our son. She invited us into her home and we were introduced to Matt's brother, which was an absolute thrill.

Many people in the village swarmed around the home and we met several of Matt's aunts, uncles, and cousins. As we pulled away from the house, I was overwhelmed with a feeling of gratitude. We had met Matt's and Nic's birth families. Words could not describe how wonderful we felt.

The meetings with Matt's and Nic's birth families helped settle once and for all, their questions of 'why' their adoptions occurred. I had always been truthful in that I didn't know the exact circumstances surrounding the adoptions but knew Romania was a very poor part of the world. The opportunity for Matthew and Nicolette to see this first hand seemed to soothe their souls.

Matthew commented that the hole in his heart was now filled and Nicolette added that she now understood why she was in an orphanage and why her adoption had occurred. She said, "I will never wonder 'why' again." These statements confirmed that our coming to Romania was, indeed, the right decision.

During our stay, we visited Corina's birth family and were so thrilled to see their excitement. Her family members kissed her at least a million times and we spent precious moments getting to know each other.

We visited all of the families again, prior to leaving Romania. During those visits, Nicolette met her birthfather and her older brother who showered our daughter with love. At lunch, Nic's birthmother kept looking at me with such affection, and her look of appreciation shining through those big brown eyes has never left my memory.

Matt's birth family treasured our second visit and both Matt and his birthmother seemed much more relaxed during this time. In fact, Matt has turned into a different child since our visit. His confidence has grown tremendously and he seems much more at ease with who he is.

I cannot tell you how happy I am that I have helped my children locate their birth families. They now know where they came from and do not have to live within walls of a fantasy kingdom. Their birth families know their children are alive, healthy, and happy. I believe that we are all much better off through meeting each other.

We have also made contact with Thomas' birthmother in Guatemala. She is happy to now know where Thomas is. I add this, because through all the adoptions, I feel God has led me to my children and now to their birth families. I often tell those around me, "You can never be over loved." I believe knowing tenderness through your parents, extended family and birth family is the greatest joy in life.

—*Annette Dambach,* New Jersey

Dear Birthdaughter

Dear Birthdaughter,
You are a woman of twenty now. In fact you are now one year older than I was when I surrendered you for adoption. I had always hoped our lives would lead us to a mutually agreeable reunion some day.

I do not look like a birthmother, whatever that looks like. I should look like a regular suburban housewife who quit her life in the corporate world to stay home with her children. I should look like your friend at church; a volunteer at her kid's school; a woman in AA recovery meetings or abuse survivor groups. I am all of these things, whatever they look like.

Perhaps more importantly is how I feel. I feel confident albeit often exhausted as I continue my healing journey. Every year it gets a little better as time continues to reduce the pain. I have been married twelve years and have two beautiful boys, but no girls. Oh how I grieved losing you once again when at the ultrasound for my second son we discovered the baby was a boy. I just assumed the universe would not be so cruel as to exempt me from having a baby girl of my own after what I had been through giving you up. But it was not to be. So shocked was I that I had to excuse myself from the examining table quickly to reach the bathroom before letting go with uncontrollable sobbing, not a common trait of mine. I adore my son who indeed did not turn out to be my daughter. That day, however, was an extremely tough one. As if to either intensify my lack of control in life or somehow ease the burden, that day landed directly on your 15th birthday; the ultrasound was on the exact hour of your birth. I had no realization of this until after the appointment was scheduled.

You never were mine. From the very moment I chose adoption, I felt to the core of who I am that you were always theirs. So when I saw your familiar face, and simultaneously felt a wide and sorrowful distance between us, it did not surprise me. I talked to you my whole pregnancy about your real mom and dad chosen by God. I never knew your parents and I never felt as though I needed to. You joined your family as you were meant to and I firmly knew it despite how broken my heart and life felt.

Today, my life is good in many ways but the road is still rocky. I suppose life should never be entirely without bumps. I have a few more major potholes that I am slowly filling that resulted from years of denying the impact of childhood abuse. Nonetheless, I am working diligently for myself and my family to heal the worst of it and move beyond. I'm working as fast as I can and when I get to the other side, I do hope to meet you there. I hope you can understand why I cannot yet begin our relationship, if indeed this is your desire.

I am not your mother but God blessed me to bring you into this world. And I was blessed again by the gift of your real parents giving you the life they have given you. They mean the world to me and no matter what happens in the future, I would never wish to hurt them in any way. Despite the fact that I never got my own baby girl, you are their daughter not mine, and that is more than O.K. It is perfect.

I do not know what a relationship might look like between you and me. I do know, when the time is right, I am willing to find out. I hope then to answer all your questions. I do so look forward to discovering what a wonderful person you are and to personally thank your parents from the bottom of my heart. May God be in your heart everyday as you are in mine.

Love,
Your Birthmother

—*Anonymous Author*

Unknown Hero

Daniel

A hero can conjure up different images for different people. For some, heroes come in the form of famous politicians or accomplished athletes. Others may envision George Washington or even Super-Man. My hero is a woman. I don't know her name or what she does for a living. Her interests are a mystery to me, as is her marital status. I like to imagine what she may look like or sound like. Sometimes, when I am walking down the street or driving in my car, I will see a woman with dark curly hair and I ask myself, "Is she my hero?" I don't know many details about her, but there is one fact about this woman that I would bet my life on — my hero knows what love is.

Roughly fourteen years ago, my mother and father had a strong desire for another child. No matter how hard they tried, my mother was unable to carry a baby. I can vividly remember the pain my Mom and Dad felt every time their attempts to have another child failed. My Mom became numb to any hope that she would have a happy ending with another pregnancy.

Disappointment led to exhaustion, which led my family to a life transforming decision: we would adopt a baby! We knew God was in control and that He would bring a child to us if this was His will.

At the same time my family was making the decision to adopt, there was a young college student making an equally profound decision. She was pregnant and weighing the important choices in front of her: Abortion, Adoption, or raise this child on her own.

My hero recognized that life is sacred and precious and that, sometimes, loving someone means letting go. She chose adoption.

I remember going to the adoption agency on May 26, 1989. A young couple passed in front of us in the hallway and I wondered who they were. Our social worker called us into her office and the same young couple entered with a baby boy in their arms. He had curly dark hair, and the cutest dimples I had ever seen. This young couple had been taking care of my new baby brother until he was ready to come home with us.

They called my baby brother "John," but my family named him "Daniel Alexander." We left the adoption agency that day with a new family member and a new hero.

Daniel is now becoming a young man who is unlike any other teenager I have ever known. He is so sweet, tender, sensitive, and loving.

He adores his family and makes us laugh all the time. Daniel's thick, curly hair is always a mess and his height is overwhelming! He still has those cute dimples that I've loved since the day he joined our family.

I hope someday that my hero will have the honor to meet this wonderful young man, my brother. Where is my hero? Could she be reading my words right now? I don't know. I do know one thing for certain, though. My hero is a brave and courageous woman who loved my little brother enough to let my family love him and raise him for her.

—*Katie Street,* Tennessee

My mother knew virtually no facts about my birth-mother and so she filled in any missing gaps with unconditional love and appreciation for the woman who gave me life. She would tell me how wonderful this woman was to have given birth to me and always spoke with great respect for her. I grew up knowing two things: I was a girl and I was adopted. To me, the adoption part was as normal and natural as knowing I was female.

I also grew up loving a faceless, nameless, unknown woman for whom I felt only positive feelings. I always felt it would be my birthmother's place to search for me, and if she ever wanted to find me, she would. Thirty-five years after bringing me into this world, I learned my gut feeling was right. It was then, that my birthmother reached out to me.

After marrying my husband, we soon learned that we were unable to have children. After coming to grips with this reality, we decided to adopt.

Our first child was a beautiful little girl adopted from the state of Texas. We named her Cara, short for Caroline, which her birthmother Christina had named her. Cara had pieces of her early life documented through pictures of her birthmother, along with a letter. She also had pictures of each day she waited in foster care for her forever family.

This was information I was never given as it pertained to my own early days as a child in waiting. I call those days 'the missing days' as I lay in a hospital in Vermont, nameless and parentless, awaiting my adoptive home. Thankfully, those gaps were filled for Cara.

I wanted Cara to honor and love her birthmother as I was taught to honor and love mine. So, pictures of Christina were hung on the wall of Cara's room where they remain today.

Four years after adopting Cara, our son Hayden joined the family. Immediately, pictures of his birthmother decorated the walls above his bed as well.

When Hayden was nearly two, I received a phone call at my home that forever changed my life. A woman on the other end named Leslie, asked how I felt about my birthmother. Instinctually, I knew what was happening.

Composing myself, I told Leslie that I always knew my birthmother would, someday, want to meet me and that I would be willing to meet her. I was asked how quickly I could move on signing consent forms. I knew at that moment, something was wrong. Ten years prior, I had requested medical history on my birthmother, which showed she endured poor health. Knowing that time was of the essence, I decided to go sign the forms the next day.

Desiring to share this experience with my two children we drove to the place of my adoption 35 years earlier. I signed the documents and then asked what my birthmother's name was. "Phyllis" was the reply.

Phyllis! I looked at my children and said, "My birthmother's name is Phyllis." An answer to a question they had so many times before asked.

As the week progressed and consent forms were signed, I discovered why there was such a rush. My birthmother was in the final stage of her life. I gathered a collection of baby pictures and sent them overnight to Phyllis.

Leaving our son with my mother on the day of the reunion, Cara and I drove to the hospital alone. My husband followed later. There we met my social worker, Dorsey Naylor. I was told that Phyllis had been very sick all winter which helped prepare us for how she would look.

I walked to the room where my birthmother was waiting and opened the door to find Phyllis in a wheelchair with her sister standing behind her. Her sister looked just like me! I immediately went to my birthmother and wrapped my arms around her chest, hugging her. I told her that my adoptive mother wanted me to deliver a message of thanks.

Over the next eight months I grew to deeply love Phyllis and to understand the love and pain she had experienced through my adoption. We spent Mother's Day and my birthday together. I visited her the night before she was to be transferred to a Massachusetts hospital to begin dialysis. This would be our last visit as Phyllis soon passed away. I was the last person to see Phyllis before she died.

My husband and I have since adopted our third child, Sam. Cara, Hayden and Sam can be sure that I will do everything in my power to lovingly fill in the gaps of their adoption stories. I am forever grateful to Phyllis for reaching out to me and filling mine.

—*Leslie C. Howard-McIntyre,* MA, LCMHC, Vermont

Dear Reader

My friend, Nancy Hardwick, wrote two of the letters you are about to read. One was written to herself, *Dear Me*, and the other to her cousin, *Dear Cousin Thrower*. Both letters are about her path of discovering whom her birthfather was. Ray Brock was his name and he, along with Alice Brock, were the inspirations behind the Arlo Guthrie song in 1967 entitled Alice's Restaurant and the 1969 film of the same name. Both became a pop-culture phenomenon, far exceeding anyone's expectations at the time.

The song and film tell of events that followed the dumping of refuse down a Stockbridge, Massachusetts hillside on Thanksgiving Day, 1965. Two young men, Arlo Guthrie and a friend—guests of the Brock's—did the dumping. The local police chief discovered the refuse and an envelope with the name "Brock" on it, and so the story begins.

For my friend Nancy, the song and movie are more than just pop-culture legend. They have assisted in helping her uncover a part of her birth heritage.

The chorus of the song goes:
You can get anything you want at Alice's Restaurant
You can get anything you want at Alice's Restaurant
Walk right in, it's around the back
Just a half a mile from the railroad track
You can get anything you want at Alice's Restaurant
(Lyrics as reprinted in "This is the Arlo Guthrie Songbook," New York, 1969, pp. 91-95)

Nancy wanted answers to the past. *Alice's Restaurant* has helped serve up some of those answers.

—*Michelle Madrid-Branch,* New Mexico

Ray and Alice Brock on their wedding day.

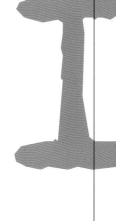

Dear Me

Nancy

In a way, I feel like I was a seed thrown into the wind and, somehow, those winds blew me to a place where I was nurtured and loved. Sometimes, the best thing about being lucky is recognizing just how lucky you are. I wouldn't trade who I am for anything in the world.

When I discovered whom Ray, my birthfather, was I knew he had given me that incredible zest and excitement for everything. Then my adoptive parents took me in, loved me, nurtured me and gave me the chance in life I needed.

Yes, the same strong feelings, strong impulses, have been a hard thing to harness and it has taken me many years to accept it and reign myself in, learning how to appreciate this gift. So many people go through life with such sadness, unaware of the joys and the beauty around them. I wake up almost everyday with such excitement and happiness. Oh, even the smallest things intrigue me.

It is so very sad that Ray's life took the course it did. He was such a creative and talented person. What a tragic wake the alcohol left behind for his children, his wives, his parents, and yes, for his own being.

I heard his singing voice on a tape and I felt his soul. I felt the power in his voice. Those are my genes too. Oh, how I wish I had known him. But, I do!

I lived by the sea and I woke up every morning to the sun over the Atlantic Ocean, just as my birthfather did. I breathed in the same salt air: Yes, I know him very well. I paint and I create and, deep within, I know I am the lucky child because I understand his pure essence, his pure soul, and his goodness. There is sorrow in the hearts of the other children. I did not have to know the pain they endured from Ray's life while he was living.

I was sitting at the round table, at Alice's house, with pictures of Ray scattered over the table. For a moment, I saw me in his face and in his smile. I was sitting at the same table where my birth-father sat. I came to find him and, in the process, I found myself as well. Tears began streaming down my cheeks and Alice patted me on the shoulder and said, "It's alright to cry." Somehow I became whole at that moment.

Time does not travel in a straight line. I cannot explain it. **I cannot explain it.**

—*Nancy Hardwick,* New Mexico

Nancy with her father,
Lester Hardwick

Dear Cousin Thrower

Nancy

Many powerful moments have taken place during my journey of adoption truth. I believe Ray is with me in spirit. I sometimes question whether this is just my spirit being found inside myself. Do we dream the dreams of our ancestors? A lot of these questions stem from being a person of adoption. I am just starting to see more clearly.

One of the big events on this journey happened when I traveled to Idaho to meet my birth sibling, Fletcher. We drove up to this magnificent lake with mountains all around. We walked and talked by the lake. I took my shoes off and began wading in the water. At the bottom of the lake I found beautiful round rocks. Slowly, I started making a rock sculpture as I spoke with Fletcher. I felt very comfortable and at ease; like we were children. It just felt right being there with him, my brother; a member of my lost tribe. As we talked about Ray and Fletcher talked about Ray's life, we were both building our rock sculptures.

Then, I found a rock that was split into two pieces. I picked the pieces up and put them together. They fit perfectly. It was something magical. I cannot explain it, except to say, I felt the rock had been waiting there for a long time, as if Ray left it for me to find knowing that when I found him, I would be whole. There was such symbolic meaning discovered at that moment. I brought the rock home where it now sits in my living room.

Later, I was given a photo of Ray sailing on the Chesapeake Bay when he was a young man. I mailed it to his children, and to Alice. For some reason, I drew a big star on each envelope. When they received the envelopes, they told me that Ray's favorite symbol was a star. In fact, a star adorned his workshop door. I feel connected to him. It is as if my birthfather is reaching out to me from beyond, in order to help me heal and be at peace.

P.S. The real stars of my life will always be my parents: Lester Hardwick and Joan Hardwick.
—*Nancy Hardwick,* New Mexico

Then, I found a rock that was split into two pieces.
I picked the pieces up and put them together. They fit
perfectly.

As I reflect on my feelings and thoughts when, at twenty-years old, I learned the results of the pregnancy test, I knew my life might change forever. When I learned of my pregnancy, I was single, in college, and very frightened. Abortion was a legal option, and anyone faced with an unwanted pregnancy can identify with the feeling of how that choice would 'take care of the problem.' But I had always felt that, once conceived, new life should be protected. I thought long and hard about the options and with the help of a wonderful pregnancy counselor, I decided adoption would be the best option for my child. The baby's father and I were not going to marry and he supported me in my choice. I always remember feeling at peace with this decision.

I made the adoption decision out of love, and at great emotional expense. I wanted to provide my baby with a stable, two-parent family that was able, willing and happy, to raise a child. At the time I was not ready or able. The laws afforded me the option of confidentiality in my decision. My privacy would remain protected unless, at a later time, a court of law determined that a good reason existed to open the adoption records. Of course, if the need arose in the future for more medical information about me, I would be happy to provide it anonymously. I knew I had to look at the long-term picture when considering my adoption decision, and took all things into consideration.

This decision was not made in an era when shame surrounded a single pregnant woman, or when adoption was cloaked in secrecy. For me, however, given all the facts and emotions I knew and felt, ongoing confidentiality was vital. When I had my baby, a precious girl, one of the nurses at the hospital said it would be better if I didn't see her. I had to disagree and I spent three wonderful, bittersweet days with my newborn. The hardest thing I ever did was put her down for the last time and say "Good-bye." But I believed then as I do today, that my choice was the best for all involved.

Immediately after the birth I was grief stricken. For the first few years following the adoption, I stayed in touch with the agency, and they provided me with confidential updates about my child's progress. Given all the emotions I experienced, it was reassuring for me to hear about my child during those early years. As time passed, my grief lessened.

I let the agency make the decision as to who would adopt my baby. I never met the adoptive parents, though I did receive certain information about them that gave me a sense of what they were like, such as their personalities, occupations, and lifestyle. The agency did honor my desire to have my child raised in a family with the same faith as mine.

After the adoption, I continued my education, was blessed with good employment, a wonderful husband, and children. The whole adoption experience shaped me in ways I never could have imagined, and lessons learned then have recurred over the years. Here are a few:

Sometimes, things happen over which I have no control.
There are consequences to every decision I make.
If the consequences seem adverse, I can still make the most of a situation.
I don't have the answer to every question.
I must accept life on its own terms, not mine. This is key.

In addition to those lessons, I find that I am far less judgmental than I was before the adoption. If someone comes to me with a problem, I am able to show empathy in his or her pain, a trait that was not so prominent in me before the adoption decision. These lessons have served me well over time and I can pass them on to others in my life. I pray that the adoptive parents have passed similar lessons on to (my, their, our) daughter.

I have always been at great peace in my decision to keep the adoption of my child confidential. I pray she feels the same and I hope she will understand and believe me when I say "Thank you for respecting my privacy. Please know that giving you life and a strong beginning were sacrifices of love, not abandonment. I remember you and will love you always."

—Anonymous Author

Unexpected Love

claire

Andrea and I sat silently trading looks while a newborn baby girl rested peacefully in a carrier between us. The clock on the wall seemed to command our attention and distract us from a meeting that was taking place in a conference room next door. Time seemed to stand still as the minutes of the clock dragged on.

Less than a week earlier, we had sat in that same room at an adoption agency in Lufkin, Texas, across from a young couple. We had been trying to adopt a baby for more than a year and this was our first meeting with the birthparents. After five years of unsuccessful infertility treatments and a miscarriage, we were now facing a new chapter in our lives. We were anxious to see how this journey would unfold.

The young couple asked to meet with us after reviewing our personal information. I suspect that hundreds of birthparents had reviewed this information and read our story over the previous year, yet for some reason, this couple chose us. What leads birthparents to select a specific couple to adopt their child is as mysterious and miraculous to me, as is life itself.

We entered that initial meeting with butterflies galore. Thankfully, they were quickly calmed by effortless, casual conversation. As the time quickly passed from morning to afternoon, we engaged in a mutual exchange of stories. Marcie and Robbie, we discovered, married as teenagers after she became pregnant with their first child.

At the time their son was born, Marcie asked the doctor to perform a hysterectomy. Due to her young age, the doctor refused and twelve months later she gave birth to a second child. Shortly after this birth, Marcie got pregnant again. Barely out of their teens with two small children and a third baby on the way, they realized it was more than they could handle, both emotionally and financially. Marcie and Robbie made the decision to place this child for adoption.

Andrea and I were fully prepared to wait for some time after this initial meeting. We were shocked when Marcie stated, "I have a doctor's appointment this afternoon. Would you like to come along?" This simple question indicated the beginning of a new life. It was apparent that Marcie and Robbie had selected us to be their child's adoptive parents.

We were going to be parents!

That afternoon, Andrea accompanied Marcie during an ultrasound and experienced her first glimpse of the baby girl who would be our daughter. During the ultrasound, Andrea heard Marcie tell the doctor that she was ready to have the pregnancy induced. A delivery date was scheduled for the following Thursday. When the doctor left the room, Marcie looked at my wife and said "I want you to be a mom on Mother's Day" which happened to be the following Sunday.

When the day arrived, Marcie allowed Andrea to participate in the delivery process and to be there when our daughter, Claire, came into the world. I entered the room shortly after the delivery and was there when Marcie handed Claire to us saying, "Look, there's your mommy and daddy."

Two days after Claire was born, we found ourselves back in the same meeting room at the adoption agency, waiting and staring at the clock whose hands did not seem to move. Marcie and Robbie were in the conference room next door where they were required by the State of Texas to formally terminate their parental rights.*

After they had completed signing the documents, we talked briefly, hugged and said our goodbyes. As I embraced Marcie, I noticed she was wearing an angel pendant that Andrea had given her, after Claire was born. This was the same pendant I had given Andrea after we suffered a miscarriage and realized we might never be parents. It felt right for Marcie to have the pendant, as she now carried a loss similar to the one we had previously felt.

As we watched Marcie and Robbie drive off together, we were amazed at how our journey was so rapidly unfolding. Less than a week before, we were all strangers. Now we were bonded for life. This young couple placed a part of themselves in our arms with complete trust, for which we are forever grateful.

—*Andrea and Steve Gerlach,* Texas
*A definition of TPR — Termination of Parental Rights — is found in the Glossary of Terms.

Opening the Windows

Carla

My daughter was adopted at birth by a wonderful couple. She lived her first thirty years not knowing about her adoption. I began the search to find her. When we connected, this new truth rocked her world. After our reunion, her parents told Carla that during the adoption proceedings, the judge had instructed them to never tell this truth.

Through our meeting, Carla was able to see for herself why she was taller than everyone else in her family. She finally understood why her hair was so curly and why she was such an avid swimmer. Carla was astonished to discover how much she looked like me and how she and I shared similar interests. We immediately bonded and had long talks about these traits of similarity.

Carla's adoptive parents were at first shocked that I had searched and found her. Then they seemed extremely appreciative that I had persevered and thanked me for opening all the windows in their house. They were surprised to see how much their daughter resembled me.

Her mother told me she had been so afraid of dying because she feared Carla would find her adoption papers in the safe deposit box. I assured her that I was just another loving person in Carla's life and would never do anything to jeopardize their precious relationship.

It has now been nine years since I found Carla and our bond is very strong. My friendship with her parents is flourishing. When Carla married, her mother insisted that I sit in the front pew with her and stand next to her in the receiving line. On Mother's Day, Carla and I send flowers to each other.

Adoption was the only option for me when Carla was born. I am so grateful that the process was in place to find her a wonderful home.

—Penelope S., New Mexico

Joshua's Valentine

Driving five hours from our home in Shelbyville, Kentucky to Murray, Kentucky seemed to last forever! My thoughts were racing and my heart was pounding. We only had about a month to prepare for this special day. Everything was ready and waiting for our new baby boy. I remember feeling so happy and excited but I was also aware of his birthmother and how she must be feeling.

I was about to become a mother, something I wanted with all my heart; but I was also a social worker with years of experience and training in the area of adoptions. I don't know whether it was my training or my heart, but my thoughts kept turning toward my son's birthmother. My happiness had come out of her great sorrow and sacrifice. She was giving me a gift far sweeter than any other — her first child.

Throughout Joshua's youth, I told him about his adoption and how his birthmother made a very difficult and unselfish decision, to place him for adoption. I wanted him to know that she loved her son enough to find him a better life than she could provide. I knew it was important for Joshua to feel good about himself, and this meant he needed to understand the sacrifice his birthmother made and to hold her with pride.

Joshua has always been a special person. He is smart, funny, emotional, handsome and very expressive. He was always on the go and loved to talk and ask a million questions. Birthdays were special times around our house, with parties, presents, cake and ice cream. It was also a time to remember Joshua's birthmother and say a special prayer for her at bedtime. We knew she was thinking of him on this day.

I understood the importance and reality of a possible reunion once Joshua turned twenty-one.

Joshua had always wanted to meet his birthmother and I had promised to help him. Not long after his twenty-first birthday, he started the steps necessary in the search for his birthmother. After eight months, with no response, I started to inquire on the progress. We had to be realistic that sometimes birthmothers can't be found, or if they are, sometimes they do not want a reunion. I so wanted this to go well for my son. Then the call came announcing Joshua's birthmother had been found! She lived in Colorado and "Yes" she wanted the reunion! Her name was Lee and Joshua found out he had three brothers and one sister.

Joshua was given Lee's phone number and planned to call her that same evening. At first he couldn't believe it was real. He was so excited and nervous. At one point he turned to me and said, "What do I say to her?" I recommended he call and say, "Hi, this is Josh." I mentioned that she was probably nervous too, and was waiting for his call. That first phone call lasted for three hours! They talked as though they had known each other for years. The words and feelings just poured out. There were tears and laughter and serious moments, all in a beautiful mix within that conversation.

Over the next few weeks we all shared phone calls, e-mails, letters and pictures. Lee sent pictures of herself and of Joshua's birthfather. Now my son knows where he gets his full black eyebrows!

Lee's parents still lived near Murray, Kentucky. They had a trip scheduled to visit friends in Louisville, on the weekend of February 14, 2004, and we planned to meet them that weekend. Joshua was prepared to meet his grandparents, but had no idea what his two mothers had in store for him.

The day we met Joshua's birth grandparents was so special, I will always remember it. My mother and my husband came along for support. We met Lee's sister, husband, and daughter. After introductions, hugs and tears, Michelle stood up and said, "Oh Joshua, we have a special Valentine for you. I'll just be a minute." Shortly after that Michelle said, "Are you ready, here it comes!" Around the corner, Lee stepped out and said, "Happy Valentine's Day Josh!"

There was not a dry eye in the room as Joshua came face to face with his birthmother! The circle of love was now complete. For Joshua and for Lee, the missing pieces had been found, and they fit perfectly. For me, my heart did not break; it had been filled with the joy and love of this reunion and for the healing that took place that day.

I realize that being a parent, whether by birth or by adoption, does not mean that we own our children. Joshua will always be my son and Lee's son too. We are all winners in this story.

—*Madeline Patricia Fluhr,* Kentucky

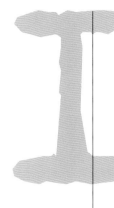

Blessings

I labored for 32 hours before giving birth to my son. I was a teenager and not able to comprehend the meaning behind my long and arduous birth pangs. Over the years, I have come to a deeper understanding.

For 32 hours, I fought against the inevitable. Knowing, in some primal way, that the moment I gave birth would be the end to a physical connection with my baby. And it was our physical goodbye.

What I have since learned, as a birthparent, is that the spiritual connection can never be severed. I have carried with me a sense of pride, knowing I am a giver of life. And I have found a sense of peace in this one simple truth: I gave birth to a beautiful child. And someday, this beauty will come back to me, somehow – someway.

The beauty re-entered my life 23 years after it left. My son, a handsome, talented, and amazing young man stepped back into my world and I have been blessed, again, with his physical presence.

It is wonderful to see the young man he has grown to be. I expected nothing less. I have always felt, in my soul, that he was okay and in good hands. Our reunion has brought the greatest joy back into my life.

I live in a state of gratitude for this gift. I am so proud to have given birth to such a special human being, with a great capacity to love. I am forever thankful to his parents for giving him everything in the world I knew he always deserved.

So many blessings, countless blessings.

—*Mary Beth Sullivan,* New Mexico

My name is Duke Boles. When I was eleven-years old my parents adopted a baby boy. We named him Daniel. Although I didn't know it at the time, he would soon be grafted into our family tree as well as into my heart. He is my brother and my friend. If I could meet Daniel's birthmother I would tell her that I am so grateful for the decision she made fifteen-years ago. She has changed our lives and completed our family. I cannot imagine life without my brother. I wrote this song for Daniel and for his birthmother. Now, I give it to you the reader.

verse 1:
She turned sixteen in early summer
and he told her he loved her so
but when he found that a baby was coming
he told her he had to go

verse 2:
In the fall she met a lady
who said there's something you should know
sometimes when you love someone
you have to let them go

chorus:
And every day I'm thankful for that teenage mother
'cause if she hadn't made the choice she did
you wouldn't be my brother
you wouldn't be my brother
you wouldn't be my brother

verse 3:
There were many times that winter
she thought of changing her mind
but she knew that she couldn't do it alone
so she had to do what was right

chorus:
And every day I'm thankful for that teenage mother
'cause if she hadn't made the choice she did
you wouldn't be my brother
you wouldn't be my brother
you wouldn't be my brother

verse 4:
A little boy was born on New Year's Day
she only saw him that one time
but she told herself she had to let him go
'cause God had a plan in mind

chorus:
And every day I'm thankful for that teenage mother
'cause if she hadn't made the choice she did
you wouldn't be my brother
you wouldn't be my brother
you wouldn't be my brother

bridge:
One day you're gonna wonder
just where you belong
but wherever you go and whatever you do
your family will be standing strong

chorus:
And every day I'm thankful for that teenage mother
'cause if she hadn't made the choice she did
you wouldn't be my brother
you wouldn't be my brother
you wouldn't be my brother

—*Duke Boles,* Singer/Songwriter, Tennessee
Single of **"Daniel's Song"** included on attached CD.

Author's note: Duke Boles is my nephew. I am proud to be
his aunt. Thank you, Duke, for sharing this adoption anthem with
the world!
—*MMB*

The Miracle of Delivery

The Miracle of Adoptive Love

Deborah Ruth

Did you know that you are part of a miracle just by being alive?

There is no doubt that life can, sometimes, deal us difficult and challenging moments. My life has been, twice, haunted by bad times. However, in both situations I found the same miracle coming to my rescue.

To explain, let me first take you back 35 years when my wife, Dorothy, and I were desperately seeking a child. Dorothy taught elementary school and I was a minister. Our community was very aware of our love for children and was also very aware of our childless state. We all know that people like to talk and those in our community did just that.

Why don't Dorothy and David have children? Is there something wrong? Whose fault is it? Are they just too busy and stressed out?

These were some of the questions swirling around our town. Finally, some church members suggested that we might adopt a child. They said it would likely take some five years to adopt. Five!! We further researched this statement and found that the "F" in five actually, and most appropriately, belongs in the word, Forms!! In fact, there were enough forms to easily keep us busy for five years. And there were more questions to answer.

Had I been true to Dorothy?
The answer was "Yes." Since our marriage I had only kissed our mothers, sisters, and the older ladies at the Senior Citizens home!

Would Dorothy and I stay together?
The answer to that was "Of course;" that is, if she could stand me.

Could we provide a proper home?
"Yes." We would never be the richest people in town, but we were stable.

Would we accept any child?

Again the answer was "Yes." With all the love in our hearts.

Looking back, I'm glad the questions were so thorough. After four months, we completed our forms and interviews and were approved to adopt. The social worker told us of a 19-year-old girl who loved her baby enough to make the mature decision to entrust her baby's care to another. We were thrilled to learn that her one-week-old baby girl would be ours immediately. Immediately! What a miracle.

Deborah Ruth looked like us. In fact, she looked better than us. She arrived with three curls on top of her head, in a gown that the nurses in the hospital bought her because she had no fancy dress to wear to meet her parents. The church generously gave us a rocking chair, where I would sing our baby girl to sleep every night. Deborah liked my renditions of Herman's Hermits and tunes by The Bee Gees. We share a love of singing.

I would learn the power of that love after a massive stroke, which left me paralyzed. I was in a Nashville intensive care unit, unable to move or talk. My thoughts were scrambled and I remember thinking that my life was over as I was no longer capable of providing for my family or doing the things that made life enjoyable.

I prayed and then heard a beautiful sound that I recognized right away. Sweet sounds of singing permeated my ears as I heard Deborah's voice. My daughter flew in to be by my side and comforted me with singing. I struggled to sing along and then found my thoughts becoming clearer, as my words became more intelligible.

My daughter helped me learn to sing again. And singing was, I believe, the bridge that brought me from the world inside my mind to the world of reality.

Adoption is a miracle. I've been blessed, and yes saved, by that miracle twice in my life.

God's love is expressed both in the vastness of the universe and in the song of a little baby girl: my girl, Deborah.

—*Dr. David R. Davis,* Tennessee

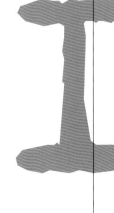

I was at work when the call came in June of 1987. "Hello, this is Sherry," said the voice on the line, "and I'd like you to be the parents of my child."

I was in complete shock, but was able to offer some garbled words of enthusiasm. I immediately contacted the social worker and made arrangements for my husband, Larry, and me to meet Sherry. The thought of meeting the woman carrying the child we would adopt made me extremely nervous. I was so afraid that Sherry would not take to us.

My fears were put to rest as our first meeting went very well. It was at that time, we discovered Sherry would be delivering in about one week. One week!

The entire adoption process started an emotional bond with our future child. I should explain; in order to adopt, one does not just fill out an application and send in a deposit. My husband and I were asked many questions about our values and our goals. The adoption agency evaluated our ability to love a child, and wanted to know about our own upbringings to help determine what our parenting attitudes would be.

We also had to reveal our incomes, submit a financial statement, health insurance policies, get medical clearance, provide reference letters, plus fingerprints and a criminal record check. All of this information is summed up in what is called a "home study"* and is required by state law.

As I reflect on the adoption process, it was similar to being pregnant yet much more. Not only were we 'expecting' a child but we really had to question our motives, individually and as a couple, for wanting to become parents. In all, it was a very emotionally fulfilling experience.

Larry and I were elated when Michelle was born. We visited with Sherry in the hospital one day after the delivery. Once again, I became a bundle of nerves as I was about to hold our new baby. I knew very little about feeding an infant or even holding one, for that matter. As I think back on the course of events that day, it must have been quite comical to see the nurse trying to show me the very basics of infant care.

The powerful mix of emotions I felt, while sharing Michelle with her birthmother on that day was awesome. On one hand, Larry and I were in love with our beautiful baby girl and so happy to have reached the important goal of parenthood together. On the other hand, as a woman, I also felt the deep emotion Sherry was experiencing.

This was a vulnerable time. Michelle, who is one-eighth Native American, had to be in foster care while we worked our way through the legalities of the Indian Child Welfare Act* (under which the Tribe must approve the adoption plan). Those two weeks felt like an eternity to me and I really do not know how I would have survived without the loving support of Michelle's foster parents.

Ours was an open adoption* which, for some, may sound a little concerning. We found that mutual openness is actually very freeing. Sherry knew with whom Michelle would be raised, and Larry and I had the unique honor of meeting the woman who gave us the beautiful gift of being parents to our daughter. As for Michelle, some may argue that knowing one's birth parents could be confusing for a child. I can only believe that not knowing the people who gave you life would be more confusing. Michelle's biological heritage is part of who she is. We honor that. Our daughter is now 16-years old and recently became a member of her Native American Tribe.

Our duty to Michelle is not to own her but to help her grow and find happiness of her own. In the words of poet Kahlil Gibran, "We are all bows from which your children, as living arrows, are set forth." Indeed, we belong to a circle of many; we are connected.

—*Judy Aron,* New Mexico
*Definitions of Home Study, Indian Child Welfare Act, and Open Adoption can be found in the Glossary of Terms.

A Double Blessing

Sonrisa & Cristal

The phone call came a few minutes before 5 p.m., "Mrs. Garcia, this is the adoption agency and we have three-month old identical twin girls for you."

I couldn't believe my ears! It had only been three months since my husband, Jerry, called a 1-800 number in the telephone book to inquire about the adoption process.

We had already been blessed with two biological children; Anhel was 14 years old and Bonita Flor was 10 years old. Jerry and I wanted more children and because of medical reasons, I was told I should not carry anymore.

We were instructed to respond by 7 p.m. that same evening. Anhel, Flor and I waited outside by the driveway for Jerry to come home from work. He claims he knew something exciting was happening due to the huge smiles on our faces.

"We have babies, we have babies!"

We couldn't help but blurt out the news at the same time. Within a two-hour period, I saw my family go from four members to six.

Today, twenty-three years later, I can still feel that warm, crystal-clear summer night, with its bright moon smiling on us as we talked about traveling 200 miles the next morning, to pick up our girls. It was that night when we chose names for the girls. One would be named Cristal (crystal) and the other would be named Sonrisa (smile).

When I first met my babies, my heart felt so big I thought it would burst with joy. As I looked around, I saw my family at my side, complete now with our new additions. In that moment, I understood fully that we were the chosen ones.

Jerry and I had not spoken of our adoption plans to family or to friends. We did not know if an adoption would materialize and, at 40 years of age, we thought the odds were likely against us.

So the evening we arrived with our twins, we called our friends and family to tell them the news and were they ever surprised. Soon, there was a revolving door at our home as people came to meet the twins. I heard someone say, "Oh, we are from Kansas." I looked up at my son, Anhel, and he replied, "I saw them going down the road and I invited them in to see my sisters!"

Everyone welcomed Sonrisa and Cristal with open arms and were a tremendous support. Some brought clothes and baby furniture. One neighbor gave us free goat's milk for a year!

I was a stay-at-home mom when the twins began school. This allowed me to volunteer on projects which continued throughout their education. The twins were in sports and school clubs and devoured every challenge that was put on their plate. "No Fear" seemed to be their motto.

The fortitude of the twins helped keep us all going when the tragedy of our lives occurred. Anhel was killed in an automobile accident in 1998. Their strength guided us through the pain.

The girls earned scholarships to play basketball in college and graduated in 2004. Sonrisa earned a Nursing Degree from Long Island University and Cristal graduated with a Business Degree from the University of New Mexico.

I am so grateful for the gift I received 23 years ago. The twins have always seen that our home is flowing with laughter, love, brightness and happiness.

They are my double blessing: the babies of my heart.

—*Elvira Garcia,* New Mexico

Adoption, What A Joy!

Adoption is every bit as exciting as giving birth! Both are gifts from GOD.

My husband, Billy, and I have been blessed with three children. After our first two years of marriage, I gave birth to a handsome baby boy with enormous blue eyes and reddish-blonde hair. Three and a half years later, I gave birth to a second handsome baby boy with enormous blue eyes and a head full of brown hair. Both of our boys totally captured our hearts and, as a mother, the depth of my love consumed me.

At twenty-five years of age, I underwent a hysterectomy and then experienced a feeling of devastation that is impossible to describe with words. I wanted, with all of my heart, to have another child – a little girl. For several years, I told myself to be thankful for what we had been given and to accept the reality that I could no longer bear a child.

Adoption began weighing on my heart and I started connecting words and actions to my desire. Billy is a pastor and we both believe fully in the power of prayer. We began praying for a baby girl to complete our family.

The Texas adoption agency we were working with gave us little hope. Ten families were on the waiting list ahead of us, and six of those ten were asking to adopt a girl. Our prayers increased!

We continued on our course and began the process of interviews and home study. Our boys were thrilled with the possibility of adopting a little sister and they expressed those feelings during the home visits. Our home study was passed with flying colors and we became the eleventh family on the waiting list. We settled in for what we believed would be a lengthy wait.

After only a few short months, we received a phone call from an agency worker stating that a young woman had given birth to a baby girl. Since her background check so paralleled ours, the agency was pushing us to the top of the waiting list. I thought my heart would leap from my chest!

Let me share my feelings throughout this time of great anticipation.

As I carried our sons in my womb, I loved them. I constantly thought about them and tried to envision what they looked like and what their personalities would be like. As I waited for my baby girl, I loved her too and constantly thought about her. I tried to envision what she would look like and what her personality would be like. I carried her, not in my womb but in my heart.

When our baby girl was eleven days old, we went to meet her. Words fail me! It was as if God placed in our arms a beautiful and priceless gift of love, wrapped in a pink blanket. As with our boys, that incomparable love of a mother engulfed me. As I looked into her beautiful face, she captured my heart, and the hearts of everyone in my family.

At eleven years of age, our little girl came to me and said, "Mom, will you tell me all about the adoption?" With a fast beating heart, I told her all that I knew. Afterwards, she asked if there were adoption papers she could review. Her father gave them to her and she walked off to her bedroom to read them. The papers were very cold and detached and only referred to her as "Said Child."

A few minutes passed, and our delightful daughter came out of her bedroom, dropped the papers on the coffee table and then headed off to the kitchen. My husband and I called out to her, "Well, what do you think?" She stuck her head around the corner of the freezer and with a big grin replied, "I think 'Said Child' will have some ice cream."

I cannot imagine life without our princess. She has become such a beautiful young woman and we are very proud of her. Adoption is every bit as exciting, full of wonder and love as is giving birth, for both are priceless gifts from God. What a joy!

—*Dee Smith,* Tennessee

When Madison says "Ma Ma"

madison

Is there any greater gift than receiving the extreme blessing of a child? From this mother's point of view, there is not. My husband, Glenn, agrees when I say that giving birth to our three children was the most wonderful, life-changing event imaginable. Two girls and a boy, EmiLee, Sarah, and Cole, added such a powerful dimension to our lives, giving us unconditional love and teaching us so much about what is truly important.

Just when I thought this mother's heart could love no deeper, we brought home our youngest daughter, Madison, through adoption.

Madison is a beautiful little girl who joined our family at the age of eight days. My little girl is African American and came into this world with Down Syndrome.* She is tremendously precious in this way.

Madison was born with severe heart defects and because her sweet heart literally had holes in it, she was unable to gain weight as newborns normally do, and was considered a "failure to thrive" child.

Her heart was working so hard to pump blood throughout her little body that it gobbled up most all of the calories that she took in. Just before Madison turned six months old, she underwent heart surgery at Boston Children's Hospital and the doctors successfully repaired the problem. She's gained weight ever since!

Today, Madison is eighteen months old and is a happy and very healthy little girl.

Yes, she thrives!

Madison is becoming very strong and is trying her best to talk. She's crawling, and is even beginning to pull up and walk along our furniture. It has been a tremendous relief for us to experience Madison's good health and to be free of the worry about her heart that once filled our every thought.

We've been so incredibly blessed by receiving this sweet little girl
into our lives,
into our hearts,
into our family.

We are so thankful for having the opportunity to have experienced pregnancy, labor, and delivery. But, when one receives a child because that child is 'chosen'. . . it offers such a different warmth to one's soul.

There is a unique feeling that I carry with me where Madison is concerned and I thank God everyday for this amazing gift. I also thank Madison's birth family for their strength, courage, and ultimately, for the little girl who has reserved such a special place in my heart.

What did I ever do to deserve such a beautiful blessing?
Madison has taught me so much about being a mother and has triggered such a deep-rooted feeling within my spirit. Yes, she along with her three siblings, have given me a true place in this world. They motivate me to do my very best in life.

Glenn and I understand the essence of sheer happiness and joy, through the lessons of adoption. When Madison says, "Ma Ma," my eyes fill with tears of delight. We couldn't be more blessed. . .until we adopt again.

—*Marie Fowler,* Vermont
*A definition of Down Syndrome can be found in the Glossary of Terms.

One winter evening, my sister-in-law and I were discussing adoption. She has four children – three biological and one adopted. As she thought of each child, she quietly smiled and said, "Funny, I just can't remember which one is adopted."

—*Michelle Madrid-Branch,* **New Mexico**

Pay It Forward

Timothy

Deep in my soul, I have always known that adoption would personally touch my life. However, I never could have guessed how deeply and profoundly I would be impacted.

My husband and I met in 1994 and were married the following year. Eager to start a family, we were well aware of the challenges we faced, stemming from the effects of my husband's juvenile diabetes. So, while trying to have biological children, we began researching our adoption options.

Three years passed, along with several failed attempts at pregnancy. The challenges of those years were difficult to handle and hard on our hearts. It seemed that couples, all around us, were having their baby dreams come true while we waited with empty arms.

In July of 2000, I saw a posting on an online message board from a woman in our state being certified as a foster/adopt parent. My husband and I decided to revisit that option and met with a local recruitment officer.

Knowing our hearts were ready, we signed up for the required 10-week class and were extremely anxious to finally have a child in our home. We were approved as foster/adopt parents in January of 2001. Three days later, our first placement moved in.

He was a beautiful and active four-year old named Brian. Each day with Brian was an amazing learning experience and we developed a close bond with him. We considered Brian as our son, in every sense of the word.

Three months after Brian moved in, we were thrilled to receive a four-month old boy named Timothy into our lives. Now, our home was abuzz with activity and it was hard to believe that we'd spent so many years without children. We felt such joy buying toys, playing games, and changing diapers—things many parents might take for granted, but to us, they were true blessings. We greatly appreciated the opportunity to be parents. The love that filled our hearts was even greater than what we dreamed about for all of those years.

We hoped to adopt Brian, but 18-months after he came to us, he was returned to his grandmother. This is a potential hardship of fostering that one should be prepared for. We still miss him.

Timothy is a different story. On December 20, 2002, we adopted him and he became a permanent addition to our family. The elation we felt that day still fills me with emotion.

Timothy has thrived in our home. Despite a past that included physical abuse and neglect, he has grown into a healthy little guy. We have been so blessed to experience his first words and his first steps, among many other things. We always felt he would be our forever son.

Life sometimes offers up wonderful surprises, and 16-months after Timothy came into our lives, we gave birth to our daughter, Sydney. People sometimes ask if there is a difference in the way I feel about my children, birth verses adopted. I am totally honest when I respond, "Absolutely not!" We know that both of our children were meant to be delivered into our lives and that God has always had this plan for our family.

Adoption has touched my life in incredible ways. I now help others on their journey through serving on support networks, teaching classes, and carrying out home studies. Adoption has been a true blessing in my family and I wish such blessings on many others.

To my best ability, I will pay it forward, as I pray their adoption dreams come true, as well.

—*Chasidy D. Bastin,* Kentucky

Adoption

New Life Through Adoption

Courtney

Six weeks prior to completing my daughter's adoption I began having dreams of giving birth to her. In this recurrent dream I was pregnant for only a few days. There was no test to confirm pregnancy and no prenatal care. During sleep, I found myself huge with child and nearing delivery. As I lay in my bed seeking a position of comfort, my swollen body ached. My back hurt and my protruding stomach claimed the space where my curled knees typically fit comfortably. Perspiration dripped from my forehead as I sluggishly twisted to an upright position in preparation for a trip to the emergency room. In sleep, I knew I was approaching delivery of my unborn child.

After I arrived at the hospital, I was quickly assessed and whisked off to a room for giving birth. (In my waking life I am a registered nurse and have on occasion assisted with childbirth, but I have never given birth.) In these surreal surroundings, I began a long but normal delivery. The labor pains were at first slow and teasing, uncomfortable but bearable. As the hours passed, my sensations and pain deepened. I was exhausted yet singularly focused on the delivery of my baby. Once she arrived, I knew before being told that I had a baby girl. She was pink and wrinkled with curled up fingers and toes and a puff of hair. I heard the doctor tell me that she weighed 8 pounds. I pulled a little pink and white outfit from my pocket and asked the doctor to dress her in it. And, I'd brought along a special boo-boo band-aid to cover her umbilical cord. My tiny newborn daughter looked up at me and said, "Hi mom!" Our physician made a comment about not needing to spank this one since she had arrived talking.

As my daughter, Courtney, and I prepared for her adoption, part of the process for us was to seek to re-connect with her first family and to allow her to make peace with her history. She often asked questions about her birth, infancy and pre-school years that I could not answer. I told her my dream and she listened attentively and with a sense of awe as I described holding her and supporting her neck and head. Then she whispered, "Mommy is this really how I was born?"

Courtney asked me to tell her the dream again and again. Each time was as if she was hearing me for the first time. After the third or fourth telling, she asked if I had taken any pictures of her and I said, "No honey, this is what mommy keeps dreaming but it's not exactly the way it happened."

Each time I had this dream I awakened feeling that I had actually given birth to my daughter. My dream always ended in the delivery room with Courtney and me lying on a delivery table. I held her and I rocked and kissed her, while cradling and stroking her fingers, toes and lips. I was content and at peace with my little daughter. But, I was never able to get discharged from the hospital to take her home. At this point in the dream I would awaken with the feeling that my daughter had always been mine, yet with an unsettled feeling that reminded me we weren't home yet. Intuitively, I sensed that God was giving me an experience of birthing my child that was healing for both of us. I did not yet know that it would also help prepare me for a task still to come.

Two days before my daughter's adoption ceremony we discovered some pictures of her taken before she entered foster care. One was taken shortly after her birth. We found several pictures taken when she was about a month old, a picture of her first visit to Santa and one taken on her first birthday. There were a few pictures taken during her toddler and pre-school years. These concrete pictures were important to my daughter, and provided comfort to her.

In my excitement, I hung her largest baby picture in a heavily trafficked area of our home in order that everyone who visits can see it. One evening, in the presence of a guest, Courtney took the picture off the wall and hid it. I quickly realized what she had done and asked if there was something else she wanted to do with it. I suggested that maybe she wanted to keep it among her private things or hang it in her bedroom where only she could see it. Deep in thought, with her nose wrinkled up and her eyes searching mine, she headed for my bedroom. She pointed to a spot in front of my bed in my direct line of vision. "Can you put it up there, Mom?" Clearly, she wanted to be my little girl.

My dreams provided me with a deep peaceful feeling of security. They provided my daughter with the sense that she belonged to me.

—*Wilma Ice,* Virginia

Author's Note: While writing this story Courtney's name was 'Courtney Rae Johnson.' After the adoption finalization, she became 'Courtney Irene RosaLee Ice.' A fact both Courtney and her mother, Wilma, are very proud to report! —*MMB*

The Very Best
Michelle

There are times in life when emotions come full circle and one realizes the very essence of love.

My daughter was placed in my arms years ago in the United Kingdom. At that very moment she became my little girl. As time has passed, I've watched her grow, sharing her joy and her tears and never wanting anything less than the very best for the 'girl of my heart.'

And the very best came on May 9, 2002 when I witnessed my daughter give birth to her son, Christian Alexander. My grandson was now in the world and I experienced birth as I imagined it might have happened when my daughter was born.

I also experienced the emotion of understanding how very difficult it must be to give a child to someone else to raise. I am forever grateful to my daughter's birthmother for making that loving and selfless sacrifice.

As I watched my girl, now a mother, hold her son to her chest I saw a tremendous sense of fulfillment radiate from her body. Now coming full circle, my daughter, Michelle Madrid-Branch is a writer and author who works tirelessly to bring her "Adoption Means Love" message to people around the globe. She is a living example of this message. Michelle could always light up a room. I stand in awe, as I now watch her light up the world.

The very best has been discovered.

—Rosemund C. Boles, Tennessee

Michelle and Christian
photo courtesy of Cathy Maier Callahan

3.

Family Building: Globally

A Flight to Forever

Dominika

I propelled myself up the aisle to the front of the plane. Having pleaded with a tired businessman, who certainly didn't want to fly home with a child — even one who didn't speak English, I had managed to procure two seats together. In the short distance of my hurry, I imagined my newly adopted daughter in a number of situations. Certainly she would be out of her seatbelt. She must be afraid I had left her. Could she be crying? Possibly she had already left the seat into which I had secured her five minutes earlier. Maybe she had even left the plane!

Straining, I spotted her still in her seat. The relief of my glimpse calmed me. She greeted me with a happy smile, still in her seatbelt, chewing her gum contentedly. I gave her a hug and relaxed into the seat next to her. Maybe this last leg of our trip would go better. At least Dominika had kept her seatbelt on for a full five minutes, even without my monitoring.

I turned to Dominika, as I explained about the airplane seat mix-up. I wondered how much she understood of my English-Polish combination. She didn't seem worried. In fact, she looked peaceful, chewing her gum. Something wasn't right, aside from the fact that she wasn't demanding anything, wasn't fidgeting, wasn't complaining. Chewing gum? I hadn't given her any. I didn't even know she knew how to chew it! Had the stewardess given it to her? I didn't think so. She seemed preoccupied with take off duties.

Stumbling for Polish words that would fit my question, I asked Dominika, "Dzie jest?" That meant "where is?" and she looked at me quizzically. "What are you chewing? Where did you get it? I mean, dzie...?" I pointed to my mouth and made chewing motions. Without missing a beat, Dominika understood. Happy to be of service, she reached under her seat and promptly produced another hard gray object someone had once called chewing gum. Triumphantly, she offered it to me. I recoiled. "Oh, no, Dominika! Nie, nie! It's dirty! Brudne! It's not good. Nie jest dobza!" She was surprised, a little wary of my vehemence. I sighed. Always ready to ad lib as a parent, I dropped my protest. After all, she'd already chewed away any germs. I relaxed again, declining her offering more calmly, and spotted a basket of apples the stewardess was preparing for our short flight. The stewardess caught my eye. "Would she like one?" "Tak," Dominika nodded. "Coca-Cola!" she added with emphasis.

Not long after our plane left the ground, Dominika had eaten the apple. The coke was sitting on my tray, as she cuddled into my side. I reminded her that now we were in America. I talked softly to her about Dad and her new brother waiting for us at the airport in Rochester, greeting us the next time we landed. Within five minutes, she was sound asleep in my arms. I sat very still, my own body relaxing after the trials of our long journey. I felt my new daughter's presence, our physical closeness, the warmth of her body against mine.

The feeling was vaguely familiar—that deepest sense of completion, of belonging, of commitment, of love. At that precise moment, I realized that I had just delivered my daughter, for better, for worse, for richer, for poorer, in sickness, and in health, into my life, forever.

—*Emily Kochanowski Jamberdino,* New York

"You may not remember that there was once a day when we were strangers, before you learned to say, 'Mama, stay!'"

"Are you sure you want to do this?" our lawyer friend asked as he notarized documents for us. "This says you're officially her guardians — what if there is something wrong with her?" Other friends doubted us as well. "Wouldn't you rather get a baby? I read somewhere that kids who haven't been adopted by the time they are two have trouble attaching." I was at the point of tears.

For ten months we watched a video-tape showing the beautiful, smiling face of a little girl in a Romanian orphanage. Now, we were in Bucharest about to meet that little girl who was to be our daughter. When the door of the orphanage examining room opened, a girl at least four or five years older than the child we thought we were adopting walked in. Before we could open our mouths in wonder, the agent said, "No, this is not Laura, this is the oldest child in the orphanage," adding, "she's seven years old and wanted to meet Laura's mother and father."

Then, a childcare worker entered the room holding a freshly washed toddler. I couldn't help but notice how scared Laura looked as she was handed to us. We arranged to take our little girl for two afternoons, prior to finalizing the adoption, so that we could get to know each other better before flying home. The second meeting went much smoother. Laura reached out her arms for us while being carried back to her orphanage for the last time.

I will not deny some of the fears I had when we first brought Laura back to our hotel room. She didn't speak at all and walked with a side-to-side motion, reminiscent of those rocking children seen in orphanage videos. I noticed, though, that after holding her hand and walking with her down the hallway of our hotel, she began to walk a little better. Two days later, in the New York airport, Laura was running!

From that moment on, Laura has continued to soar. An evaluation showed she was right on target in motor skills but quite behind in language. We began speech therapy right away. A hearing test proved she had fluid behind her ears. Surgery was scheduled and an hour after having ear tubes implanted, Laura began to speak and she hasn't stopped since. We placed our daughter in an enriched daycare program to help with communication skills. She began kindergarten, on schedule, just ten days after her 5th birthday. Laura was evaluated and placed in the highest-level language arts group, which should put to rest the myths of adopted children and school performance!

"Mommy, can you read me, *How I Was Adopted*?" Laura loves to listen to adoption stories and loves to watch the video we took in Romania. She often tells people she is adopted and doesn't seem to notice the surprised look on their faces. They're surprised because Laura looks so much like us and because everything about her dispels the adoption myths so many people have heard.

Outgoing and energetic, Laura seems to attract attention wherever she goes. In fact, babysitting for Laura inspired our neighbors to adopt their daughter! As I watch my five-year old do arabesques and chasses in dance class, I realize that all of her potential might have gone to waste if it were not for adoption.

That's when my mind drifts back to the seven-year old girl we met in the Romanian orphanage. As the oldest child in the orphanage at that time we were told that if she wasn't adopted within the next two or three years, she would either be placed in an institution or put out on the streets of Bucharest. I always experience a profound sense of sadness as I wonder, "What happened to her potential?" It is likely that I will never know. A deep sigh escapes my body as I think, "How I wish we could have afforded to adopt her as well."

Then, my mind drifts back to dance class and my little girl. Laura is the youngest child in her dance school. As she completes a complicated solo before my eyes, I see the magic of transformation.

Laura and I snuggle at night and make up for the time that we didn't have when she was a baby. As I hold her in my arms, I softly sing the words to my most recent song about adopting my beautiful daughter:

"When I lay beside you, there's a power, I understand…with my arms around you, I feel eternity in my hands."

—*Bonnie Abrams Rich*, New York

I was a small girl when my mother told me I was adopted. Though I was too young to remember her exact words, I will never forget my feelings. I felt sorry for my friends who weren't adopted. My mother had just told me what, by the age of seven, I had already felt; that my parents loved me unconditionally and that they had ached with longing for a child.

When I grew old enough to understand my birthmother's role, I realized that I had been doubly blessed. A girl who couldn't raise me had loved me enough to give me to someone who could. This selfless person knew that motherhood is more than playing house and that her ultimate responsibility was ensuring the best for the baby she had brought into the world.

In 1964, I visited the New York World's Fair. I was intrigued by an exhibit about children from other countries called, "It's a Small World." This experience would hold an even more profound meaning, later in my life.

As an adult, I found myself under the care of an infertility specialist. Though he outlined several treatment options for my husband and me, our hearts were set on adoption. Three years later, we adopted our daughter. Four years after that, I stepped off a plane from Santiago, Chile, to place our new son in his father's waiting arms.

It was clear that adoption would run in our family. Today, I watch as my Latin American son grows up beside a Chinese girl with a lyrical Italian name and Korean twins studying for their Bar Mitzvah. It seems, in ways even the World's Fair could not imagine, that it is indeed a small world after all.

I once heard my daughter tell my son, "I'm half Irish and half Italian." Then she added, "You're half Irish and half Italian and half Chilean." You may doubt our math, but never doubt this: we are a family.

—*Rosemary C. McDonough,* Pennsylvania

Perceptions

I was recently pre-boarding a flight from Albuquerque to Phoenix. A family stood waiting in front of me: a Caucasian mother and father with their sweet Hispanic infant and two adorable African American toddlers.

This "diverse" family was receiving many curious stares from others in the airport. You could see the questions looming in their heads as they tried to sort out to whom these children belonged.

A stewardess then asked the question so many waiting in line wanted to verbalize, "Are these children YOURS?" The parents' responded, "Yes, these are OUR children. We are their adoptive parents."

The stewardess looked perplexed by this answer and replied, "You must be very special people to do something like this." Her statement catapulted me back to my own childhood.

I am a person of adoption. Many times as a child, others would look at my fair-skinned parents and then look at my olive-toned skin and ask where it was I came from. After being told of my adoption, these same people would add how special my parents were to take me in, never once commenting on how fortunate my parents were to have me in their lives.

Comments like these have a strong impact on youngsters. Our skin tone goes only skin deep. Beneath a rainbow of human complexions, we all have hearts that pump blood of red.

Adoption enhances the lives of everyone involved: no matter the race, the gender, or the age. It knows no boundaries and sees no racial differences. This is sensitivity training we all can use. Perhaps our reply to those who adopt should be: "How blessed is this family!"

—Michelle Madrid-Branch, New Mexico

"We have a boy for you," the Director of the orphanage told us. She continued, "He's had a cold so he does not feel well and he may not respond to you right away." I immediately began thinking of all the children in institutions around the world who, by no fault of their own, are forced to comfort themselves when they are unhappy and learn to rock themselves on their own, in cribs often shared with other children.

I told myself I would show no alarm when I first met our son and would not comment on the lack of hair on the back of his head from being left to rest in a crib for long periods of time. I would look beyond the sores and scabs he would surely have, and see our little boy.

I looked over at my husband and knew he was thinking how he would love our son even if he were slow to show us affection. Together, we would work tirelessly to get our son on the correct developmental level through educational games, reading, and singing songs. Clark and I spent so many months researching books and articles on International Adoption, and so we felt prepared to handle any challenges that might arise.

As we waited, our translator, Luda, noticed our worried faces and tried to comfort us in her best English. "If he isn't here," she said, "we will take the micro-bus back to Kiev and return to the Adoption Center tomorrow," adding, "there are other orphanages." This information did not reassure us, but my faith told me we were in the right place.

If this little boy was our son, we would find a flat to rent in Kremenchu, hire a lawyer, and complete the adoption process. Clark and I were ready to leave the Hotel Kremen, and settle in a place with a kitchen and, hopefully, hot water to bathe with.

Then, the doors to the office we were waiting in flew open and I saw his face. I will never forget that moment!

Our son was very pale, either from being ill or from lack of outdoor activity. His gray eyes were huge as he looked up at me and smiled. I looked at my husband as I stood up and made my way to the door. As I held out my arms, my son showed me that he already had teeth and then he came to me. I held him and he never cried or tried to pull away. He was responding to me beautifully!

Our precious child put his arms around me and then put his head on my shoulder. I sat down on the office couch and began counting his fingers and his toes. He was perfect!

Clark and I immediately began telling our son about his home in America and about family members and pets. I knew that this was the first time in his fifteen months of life to hear English, but I felt he understood every word. We began passing our son back and forth and whispered sweet secrets to him: We spent many days and months in anticipation of being a family. All the minutes of your life spent waiting for us, please know, we were looking for you.

It was very hard to leave our son at the orphanage that day, but it was also very exciting as we walked out of the building as parents! Clark and I went to the orphanage every day until the adoption process was finalized. Luda rode with us on the day we picked up our son for good. Ours was her first adoption to facilitate and we had created a deep bond.

The orphanage workers were teary eyed as they kissed our little boy goodbye. They kept telling him how lucky he was to be leaving Ukraine and going to America to live. I will always know that Clark and I are the lucky ones because we found our son, SAM!

—*Clark and Patricia Parker,* Mississippi

Author's note: Clark Parker and I were childhood friends and sometimes spoke of my adoption. Thank you for listening, Clark! It's nice to know adoption has linked us together again, so many years later.

—MMB

A Journey to Glistening Snow

Kira

We are Janice, Scott, Kyle and Kira Olson. We live in a small town in Northwestern Ontario, Canada and this is our adoption journal.

"Mom, is it ready?" I finish preparing my children for their bath as they wait anxiously by the tub. "Okay, Kyle, get in." Kyle and his little sister, Kira, love being in the tub, especially when they're together. It took awhile to get Kira accustomed to bath time, but now she adores it. As laughter fills the bathroom, I get an overwhelming sense of joy. I gaze at my children who are so happy and my eyes fill with happy tears. The journey was a long one, but worth every setback and challenge. I watch my son smile at his sister, who overcame so much to join our family.

Scott and I married in 1993 and always discussed adoption as a way to build our family. In 1995, our son Kyle was born and our lives changed, so much for the better, that we knew we wanted more children. Two years later, our lives turned in a new direction as we were told, for medical reasons, that another pregnancy would put me at high risk.

I subscribed to Adoption Helper magazine and was intrigued when, in the first issue, there was an article highlighting adoptions from Vietnam. I contacted the recommended agency in Ottawa and, within hours, received an e-mail saying an information package was on its way.

A home study* was completed and in August of 1999 our dossier was off to the adoption agency. In September, the dossier was sent to Vietnam. A month later, I was reading a posting on available babies in Vietnam. Not knowing what province these children where from, and only knowing that we were waiting for our referral from the North, I decided to inquire about a baby girl named Tuyet, born on September 27th. I really didn't know if anything would come of it but I felt a connection with this baby and had to further research. Two days later,

I found out that this healthy little girl was from South Vietnam. She was an absolute doll.

Then in October, I awakened to the most beautiful e-mail I had ever received; it was a picture of the little girl who was meant to be ours. In the photo, she was sound asleep. My heart melted over her shiny black hair and perfect looking skin. She was absolutely beautiful.

I ran upstairs and blurted out, "there's a picture of our baby!" Scott jumped and almost hit his head on the ceiling when he saw the state I was in. We ran downstairs to see the photo and felt the same emotions we experienced after learning I was pregnant with Kyle! We were one step closer to expanding our family. Having a picture of this little girl filled a great void in our lives. Every time I looked at her, I wanted more and more information about her. Each morning, I would check my e-mail in anticipation of news. We decided to name our little girl, "Kira Lynn Anh Tuyet." "Anh Tuyet" means "glistening snow," in Vietnamese, and we felt it was a beautiful and appropriate name.

In early December, we were informed that Kira was fighting a respiratory infection, which was causing her not to feel well. We were extremely concerned about the seriousness of her condition and how this might affect her medical approval. After a couple of weeks that included a few scares, Kira was on the mend. In fact, she seemed to get better and better as the weeks progressed.

On February 8th, we applied for our travel visas, as anticipation filled the air. Nearly a month later, I opened the most awesome piece of e-mail ever: ***Scott, Janice, Kyle: You are approved. Come and get her. Congratulations.***

We left home on the morning of March 9, 2000 and headed for Winnipeg. From there we flew to Vancouver where we met up with my mom and stepfather, who were also making this journey to their new granddaughter, and then connected on a flight to Hong Kong. Kyle couldn't wait to meet his baby sister and see the country we had been telling him so much about.

Arriving in Vietnam, we felt overwhelmed to be so close to our baby girl. We also felt overpowered by the heat and the mobs of people on the streets.

After arriving at our hotel, excitement grew as we were about to meet little Kira. With my hands over my face, tears began streaming down my cheeks and my heart was pounding. I could hear the sound of approaching footsteps as the door opened and I saw our beautiful baby girl.

From March 12th to March 15th, we spent our days getting to know Kira and getting to know the amazing country that is her native Vietnam. We applied for her passport at the Canadian Consulate and also awaited her Visa, clearing us to leave the country. It was now time to leave Vietnam.

Kira is such an amazing little girl and we are so proud that she is our daughter. Throughout our journey, we have met remarkable people and experienced such remarkable places. We will never forget this wonderful adventure, and the many miles we traveled to bring Kira "Glistening Snow" Olson, home.

—*Janice, Scott, Kyle & Kira Olson,* Canada
*A definition of Home Study can be found in the Glossary of Terms.

Art Buchwald is, without a doubt, this country's premiere political humorist and satirist. He is, also, one of my favorite commentators on the human condition.

Born in 1925, he left home at seventeen and joined the Marines. Upon returning to civilian life, he enrolled at the University of Southern California and became managing editor of Wampus, the USC official magazine. He also wrote for the college newspaper and a variety show called, *No Love Atoll.*

In 1948, Mr. Buchwald left USC and used a $250.00 check he received as a war bonus, to purchase a one-way ticket to Paris. He began writing for Variety magazine and then was hired on at the editorial staff of The New York Herald Tribune, (European edition).

His column, *Europe's Lighter Side,* began recruiting loyal fans on both sides of the Atlantic Ocean. He soon reached legendary status.

Mr. Buchwald has carried with him a "go anywhere" mentality to gather information for his stories. This is an attribute I would admire and imitate through my own journalism career. He marched in a May Day parade in East Berlin, chased goats in Yugoslavia, and traveled to Turkey for an up-close and personal impression of a Turkish bath.

Art Buchwald's columns appear in newspapers around the world and he has authored some 30 books, including one of my favorites, *I'll Always Have Paris,* (Putnam, 1995). He is the recipient of the Pulitzer Prize for Outstanding Commentary and was elected to the American Academy and Institute of Arts and Letters.

Mr. Buchwald is an adoptive father of three. Joel, Jennifer and Connie were all adopted internationally.

Art Buchwald has contributed, for this book, a wonderful memory of bringing Joel home. It is in true Buchwald style: witty and to the point, and I must add, an honor to include within these pages.

Mr. Buchwald, as an author, journalist, and a person who was adopted internationally, I thank you for sharing this adoption moment, from the pages of your life. I salute you, sir.

—*Michelle Madrid-Branch,* New Mexico

Mr. Buchwald is an adoptive father of three. Joel, Jennifer and Connie were all adopted internationally.

photo courtesy of Art Buchwald

An Irish Adoption

Joel

My three children, Joel, Jennifer and Connie were all adopted when we were living in Europe: Joel from Ireland, Connie from Spain and Jennifer from France.

At the time they were adopted, we had to cut through international red tape to get them. In Ireland, we chose a beautiful baby boy. Unfortunately at that time, there was a big ruckus on the Emerald Isle about children leaving the country. A regulation was passed to forbid these children passports to leave.

The Irish gave me a bad time. Luckily for me, the P.R. man for TWA (Trans World Airlines), who was a friend, heard about my difficulties. He smiled and said, "Don't worry, I went to school with the Minister of Foreign Affairs." He picked up the phone and said, "John, good to talk to you. So we have a golf game on Sunday?" (Pause) "Oh, by the way, I have a little favor to ask. Can I get a passport for a little tyke who this lovely couple wants to take back to America? I'd appreciate it very much and I'll see you on the golf course."

In two days, I got Joel a passport and I got out of Ireland as fast as I could, in case they changed their minds!

The circle is now complete. When he was small I took care of Joel. Now he takes care of me.

—*Art Buchwald,* Washington, D.C.
Syndicated Humorist & Satirist, Author and Pulitzer Prize Winner

A precious moment with the Buchwald children.

For eleven years, I prayed and prayed for a baby. I wanted children so badly and my arms felt so empty. Then a series of events began to change my life. My sister's friend, from Chile, asked me, "Tell me about your children. How old are they?" Ouch, that hurt. But as the evening passed, she began to help me dream. She told me about children in an orphanage near her hometown; children that nobody in the world seemed to want.

Four months later, my husband and I, along with my new friend appeared before a judge in Temuco, Chile who said, "Twin baby boys. Go look." My Spanish wasn't strong and I said, "*por favor repetin,* please repeat." I simply couldn't believe my ears. I might have a chance to adopt not one, but two boys!

We went to the orphanage where some twenty infants were housed. The twin boys were six-weeks old and had been born two months premature, weighing less than four pounds each. They were also malnourished. One of the babies had meningitis and we were told he'd never walk and would probably die. The other baby had a heart problem. We could have asked for any of the children in the orphanage but the twin baby boys haunted us with their eyes.

As I toured the orphanage, I kept going back to these tiny and sick little babies. They would have so much to overcome in their lives. They needed so much help. Out of all the mothers in the world, these baby boys chose me. I fell in love.

One of my boys lost his ability to drink from a baby bottle because the muscles in his mouth were undeveloped. I fed him with an eyedropper, slowly placing a drop or two of milk in his mouth. Then, when he was four-years old, my little guy felt sad because he couldn't drink from a straw like other children. I went to the library and checked out numerous science books to learn about liquid, straws, and physics. I discovered that if you cut a straw shorter, it takes less force to bring the liquid through. We cut the straws and my son was so happy because he could drink like everyone else. As his mouth muscles grew stronger, the straws were lengthened.

My son with meningitis experienced problems with his balance. We became creative in our attempts to help him. So creative, that neighbor children came over just to play with us. Catching a ball was hard, so we hung a lighter one, from the ceiling of the living room, and gently swung it back and forth, learning to play catch.

When physical therapy became too expensive for us, we learned how to ice skate and this opportunity strengthened both of our boys and provided them with a sport that, to this day, they love.

My twin boys are now men and at twenty-one years of age they both attend prestigious universities, with the help of scholarships. Both have overcome their health problems and even play ice hockey! They hold leadership positions at their college campus and volunteer in the community. They also mentor other children who are adopted from South America.

God does answer prayer. He gave me babies to hold and he gave my twin boys a new chance at life.

—*Susan Horner,* Colorado

Miracle Children

Latessa & Jaimen

In the summer of 1984, I found myself divorced. Yet, I still carried a deep desire to share my life with children. For me, it was not important to have a 'biological' child, and so I attended the Vermont Adoption Fair.

My single status left me feeling rather vulnerable. I attended adoption workshops and kept primarily to myself. As I walked around, I noticed a room marked 'India' and went in. There I met an adoption social worker, Alice Siegriest, who was packing up from her long day of workshops on foreign adoption. Her focus was the International Mission of Hope Orphanage in Calcutta, India. As we talked, I shared my hope of adopting a baby and then shared my perception that single parents could only adopt older, handicapped or emotionally challenged children. Somewhere down deep inside, I thought adoption was not an option for me. Alice replied, "The countries of Columbia, Brazil and India allow single parents to adopt babies. India has a program where single parents may adopt infants; the only requirement is that there is a 'loving home' for the child." She added that, currently, India was closed for adoption. However, when it opened back up, she promised to give me a call. I wrote my name and number on a napkin, handed it to Alice and we departed.

My family, who lived far away, offered little support or blessing for my plans or desire of adopting. My father thought I was crazy. My brothers questioned how I could raise a child on my own and feared I would be less likely to re-marry. They would ask, "What man will want to take on a single mom and her child?" At that point, I thought it best to keep from my family that I had every intention of adopting not one but two children.

There were many obstacles along the way. Still, my longing to adopt remained so strong that nothing would stand in my way. During the months of short daylight, between November and February, I went through "the dark night of the soul." My imagination ran wild as visions of the best and worst possible scenarios for my future played out. It was both a painful and exhilarating experience.

Late January brought with it extreme clarity. I did want to adopt and I wanted to adopt from the country of India. In early February, I was away at a work conference. I called the Vermont Children's Aid Society and left a message for Alice stating, "When India opens I definitely want to get on the list." You can imagine my surprise when I got home a week later and found a message on my dining room table from my roommate. It read, "Alice from Children's Aid called. India is open. Interested?" The phone message was dated February 1st. Our messages had crossed. Vermont had a quota of twenty children. Nineteen families were signed up and I was next on the list. I was ready.

Natessa, at four months old, arrived home to me in April of 1986. She weighed eleven pounds. Jaimen, also at four months old, arrived home to Natessa and me in June of 1989. He weighed seven pounds. When the children were eight and five years old respectively, another miracle happened. Daniel Wetmore, a kind, sweet and wonderful man joined our lives and became their loving father. Dan adopted Natessa and Jaimen after we married in 1997: a Cinderella story to be told another time.

A Colorado woman started the International Mission of Hope in Calcutta. Western doctors have visited this orphanage to study the lives of babies from date of conception to their premature births. Most deliveries are induced at seven months due to a lack of nourishing food. Also in India, out-of-wedlock pregnancy holds a severe social stigma. To avoid controversy and shame, pregnancies are induced early when young, unmarried women begin to show.

The infant mortality rate in India reaches a staggering eighty-percent during monsoon season. The deaths are linked to dirty water. Western doctors conclude that there is no known medical reason why any of these babies should have lived. Because of this, the orphanage stamps "Miracle Baby" on the paperwork of each surviving child.

I always dreamed of taking my children back to India, in order for them to experience their homeland. Every time Dan and I began planning a trip, both children would say they did not want to go. Natessa would say, "Mom, why would I want to go to India? I am happy here. I am thankful that I am adopted. I have a great life here with everything I could ever want. If I was in India, I would probably be living the life of a street girl." Jaimen was simply afraid to go. His picture of India was that of a land filled with cobras slithering the streets. As the years passed, we shared friendships with other adoptive families who have children from India and we learned about the country through books, artifacts, pictures and other people's stories.

In 2004, a special opportunity came out of the blue. A man in our community wanted to take six high school students to the International World Social Forum and the International Youth Camp in Mumbai, India! Natessa was up for going and I welcomed the opportunity. We raised $10,000 through the generosity of our friends and neighbors. Natessa and I, along with seven others, were going to India!

The flight was 18-hours long when the wheels of the plane touched the airfield in Mumbai. At that moment, I felt the presence of Jaimen's and Natessa's birth parents so strongly that I found myself sobbing. My tears were also of joy because my life's dream of going to India was now a reality. I was so grateful and felt extremely overwhelmed.

My experience of India was one of connection. I felt like I walked through a womb and was delivered whole as a woman, mother, and human being. It was different for Natessa, however. The third day in Mumbai, we were at the campsite when Natessa suddenly blurted out in front of everyone, "This is not at all what I expected it to be. I feel no connection here, and I'm ready to go home!" I was shocked. When I asked why she felt this way, Natessa could not tell me. We were all jolted by the immense poverty we were seeing. So that must be the reason for Natessa's remark, I thought. Then I realized it was perfectly understandable that she felt no link to her native land. She was born in India, but grew up an American. She must have been feeling a lot of pressure. Dan and I had wanted her to feel something for her homeland. I said to Natessa "It's perfectly fine not to feel any connection."

During our visit, Natessa spent time, sang, learned and laughed with thousands of Indian teenagers. All things considered, she had a wonderful trip. She feels complete with her visit to the land where she was born and says she does not need to return to India. As for Jaimen, he is older now and I don't think he is plagued by visions of cobras anymore. He still chooses not to go to India. Time will tell.

I love my children and my husband. For us, a dream came true; one that continues to unfold each day of our lives. I am thankful to all who have shared the hardships and the happy times and for the villagers of Montpelier who helped raise our children. Without them it would have been so lonely.

People used to say to me "What a wonderful thing you did to adopt these children." I would respond "It is I who have received the most love, happiness and blessings." As the stamp on their paperwork explains: Jaimen and Natessa are miracle children. They are miracles for surviving and miracles in our lives.

—*Josephine Romano,* Vermont

To My Daughter's Birthmother

Alia ManLi

Alia ManLi

One of the realities of adopting a child from China is that there is no information about our daughter's birthparents. Due to complex laws and circumstances the children are usually abandoned without any note telling anything of their family or history.

In our Western way of thinking, we make an erroneous assumption that the Chinese do not love or value these children; this is simply not true. Many Chinese families find themselves in an impossible situation that leads them to have to abandon their child.

Throughout this adoption process, I have found myself thinking about the birthmother of my daughter-to-be. Somehow she found the courage and strength to do the impossible and she lovingly let go of her precious child. I can only begin to imagine her sense of loss. It is because of her love that we are about to become parents. This is a gift we will never be able to thank her for, except through loving her child as our own.

As my husband and I prepared to travel to China to meet our new daughter, I wrote this letter to her birthmother.

To Alia ManLi's Birthmother,

I wanted to write to you now, before I meet this child/your child, who we will always share in the Spirit of Motherhood. Now, before I get caught up in the wonder and amazement, fatigue and joy, that surely must accompany one into first-time motherhood...I am sending this letter to you on the winds of love that created this child and the light of the miracle that will bring her into my life.
I do not want you to be forgotten in this process.

Many nights I lay awake thinking of your child / my child, wondering who she will be and what she will be like. She will not have my eyes or my husband's nose, but she will have pieces of your family tree that will blossom over time for us to discover. As I lay in the dark, I also think of you. Somewhere, a world away, you are walking through your day in China with a broken heart over the loss of your darling daughter. You, too, are thinking of this child and worrying if she is okay.

You did what had to be done in an impossible situation — hoping that your daughter would have a chance at another life, somewhere else, with people who love and cherish her. Yours was an incredible sacrifice.

You love her, and always will, because she is the blood of your blood. I love her, and always will, because she is the heart of my heart.

I will raise her to know the Spirit of you. In autumn, during the Mid-Autumn Moon Festival, we will go out into the moonlight and talk of you. We will send you good wishes and prayers on the evening breezes.

You will be a part of her life and will share in each happy moment. You will be there when she learns to ride a bike, when she graduates from high school and college, when she marries, and when her first child is born. I'll remind her that mothers always love and remember their daughters, no matter how far away they are.

I do not know you and yet I will come to know you through this child we share. As the years pass, you and I will become closer as parts of you bloom within her. I am looking forward to getting to know you through your daughter–my daughter. The debt I owe you can never be repaid; however, I promise to love this little girl, and the woman she becomes, with all of my heart. You are her nature and I promise to nurture her all the days of my life. I will take her into my heart and home and love her always. I will share her with you across time and space.

You will not be forgotten.
Humbly,
Cheryl Cutting

No one could have told me, before we decided to adopt a child, the depth and breadth of love and emotion we would encounter on this path of adoption. The process has opened my heart and my eyes in new ways. The sweet child who was placed in my arms on February 10, 2004 has changed my life forever.

I am connected to and indebted to my daughter's birthmother for the rest of my life. It is my commitment to honor my daughter's heritage all of her life.

—*Cheryl Cutting,* New Hampshire

Adoption Journal

Storey

'Adoption Journal' is written by famed novelist, Ridley Pearson. Mr. Pearson documents, in powerful detail, his journey to meet his baby girl, Storey, in China. I thank both Marcelle and Ridley Pearson for sharing the very texture of their daughter's native land with us, while also sharing their intimate thoughts on becoming a family. *—MMB*

Dear Storey,

Our trip to bring you into our family started late on a Friday afternoon and a series of plane flights that began in Hailey, Idaho and took us to Salt Lake City and Los Angeles before arriving in Guanzhou at about 7:30 AM. We had traveled for over 30 hours and we ate our first meal on Chinese soil in the Guanzhou airport. The constant movement of China's people became so apparent to us immediately – a controlled chaos filled the airport terminal, and there were enough restaurants for a small city. We flew on to Guilin, met by a guide named Bai, and spent the night at the Garden Hotel. It is difficult to describe our first impressions of your native land, our wonder at the energy of its people and near-poverty exis- tence of the people of Guilin. Our hotel looks out onto the Li River, and our room, out across the spires of karst that rise like towers from the rice patties and apartment buildings that exist cheek-to-jowl here. But the wonder for your mother and me remains that our first meeting with you is now less than two days away. All these months of waiting are compressed into just forty-eight hours, and our hearts pound in anticipation of holding you in our arms.

We have come to China two days early, mostly to adjust to the time change, but also to see a few sights before moving on to Kunming. We saw reed flute cave yesterday, and I write now from a trip down the Li River. The limestone peaks rise dramati- cally from the lush vegetation, a deep, saturated green of bamboo, pine and so many trees and plants we've never seen. The river is a murky green, like dark jade, undulating and twisting through the towers, past tiny villages and compounds, gravel spits, water buffalo, cormorants and fishermen on bamboo skiffs barely four inches out of the water. The talk between our fellow New Hope families and us varies between the impressions of the stunning scenery and expectations of our time with you. When will we see you? Tomorrow night upon our arrival, or the following day? So many questions—our hearts beating joyfully as we think of you. We have brought two duffel bags with us—nearly all of it for you: clothes, diapers, formula, food, baby carriers. Books. Tape recorders and players. All hoping to have what we need when we meet you. To make you as comfortable as possible for our long journey home.

You are joining our family. We are painfully aware of the responsibility that bears upon us. We want to make this transition for you as seamless and smooth as possible—to cherish without smothering, to provide without over-indulging, to welcome you into a family whose premise is love. Love and its enduring power, strength and calm. This country in which you live has filled us with awe. It is inspiring. Yet we know it pales in comparison to one glimpse of you, one smile, one moment in your presence.

* * *

Following our river trip we drove back to Guilin on a wide cement road that split the verdant valley in two, both sides encased by distant karst ranges almost artificial in their stage-set beauty—two dimensional, round-topped green spires, armies of them in regimented splendor. And along the roadway, reaching toward those hills, yellow-hued harvest time rice patties stitched into the dripping green patches of sprouts ripening quickly in the muggy summer air, geometric fields of still water like broken mirrors reflecting back the jagged-mouth splendor of those karsts. The challenge is to stay focused, for I am so easily distracted by the spectacular scenery that my imagination drifts unconsciously to peaceful, serene dreams of the simplicity of life here. To rise, water, plant, harvest—cycling through seasons with years falling away like autumn leaves.

Along the road, in lanes designated just for them, bicycles carry everything imaginable: rice straw, melons, sticks, rebar and brick. Here in this valley it is all brick—we pass factories, the rich red bricks stacked in perfect rows five feet high, whole fields of them awaiting mortar and attention somewhere farther up the road. A place to call home.

Everything comes back to you, dear Storey. A home. You have been treated well here—we trust that—but have yet to find a home, like those stacked bricks out in the field. Marcelle and I hope to give you the love—the mortar—to bind you to our lives, to include you in the music and the laughter we call home. To give you an older sister, Paige, who, like us, already anticipates your inclusion into our family circle. Our dinners, our family baths, our games of hide-and-seek and our bedside prayers. In this family, so much comes down to prayer.

And so, as another day slips toward night, bringing us inexorably closer to you—our purpose in this visit—we whisper prayers for our reunion with you and the magic we feel certain to follow us for all of our days.

* * *

Today your mother and I visited a "free market" in Guilin—a huge, indoor-outdoor market with no tourists—a Chinese street market for the Chinese of Guilin. We saw every vegetable, every cut of meat, egg, spice, mushroom, hatchet, dress, shoe, knife, etc. you could ever imagine. We bought your mother a black leather belt for $3 U.S.—about ⅕ what it would have cost back home.

Our guide then took us up Fobu Hill—all 325 steps—to a 360 degree view of this memorable city. The green river flowed on as it has for tens of thousands of years. Currents swirled. We were captivated by the surrounding mountains once again—our final glimpse of this dramatic place while outdoors. We cooled down some in a cave at the base, where vandalized Buddha sculptures two thousand years old stared solemnly into the hills, poetry chiseled into the ceiling walls dripping with water.

We lunched in a revolving restaurant, all of us giddy about our upcoming flight to Kunming and our meeting with our children. Bai, our guide, escorted us to the airport, and now we are in the plane: Chris, Cathy, Gary, Christina, Kara, and Di. Nerves are high. We may see you this same night! We can't wait!

All this way from home we have no idea what to expect, other than we will be met at the airport and driven to Greenlake Hotel. There is talk you may join us tonight—tomorrow morning at the latest. Dear Storey, I can't tell you how thrilled we are at this chance to be with you. We weep when we talk of you. We laugh. Chills run down our spines. We can only hope that someday these next few hours will mean as much to you as they do now to us. A beginning. A treasure. A family. Your elders say "a journey begins with but a single step." We, the four of us— Paige, you, your mother and I—now take that first step toward a future together. We unite and we move

We, the four of us—Paige, you, your mother and I— now take that first step toward a future together.

forward. Your grandfather likes to quote a passage from the bible; coincidentally your mother read this same passage aloud this morning, and it seems so appropriate: 'This is the day the Lord hath made, let us be glad, and rejoice in it.' We are rejoicing, dear soul, with every passing minute drawing us closer to you. Rejoicing, at the strange and wondrous journey that has led us here.

* * *

Today was an emotional ride into all of our futures. We started out quite early, leaving the hotel and crossing a wet road, heading over to a government complex where a pair of armed guards would not allow us inside, their gloved hands gesturing us back. We moved across to a parking area where we were made to wait. We were met a few minutes later by an escort and allowed to enter the complex. We walked a short distance to a very old, very dilapidated building and we climbed four flights in the dark, the only light through windows which no longer held any glass. The hallways too were dark and gloomy, though the occasional office was lit brightly and had adequate furniture inside. We walked down this extremely dark passage and were shown into quite a nice room with a long oval table and many chairs. We sat down at this table, China's red flag in metal on the wall, the windows a filthy gray. Emotions ran high as we were made to fill out forms and complete statements about how we intended to care for you as a member of our family. And then, in the middle of all that, the caretakers paraded in bearing the babies in their arms. Adorable, bright-eyed little children as filled with expectation as the adults who had come to take them across the ocean. Tears sobbed down onto this great oval table as the forms dragged out, all of us eager to leap from our seats and go claim our daughters. Cameras flashed. More tears. Couples hugged and squealed as we all identified our children from the photos we had cherished all these long months. No longer Kodachrome. Living. Breathing. More tears.

Our organizer, a wonderful woman name Lin, walked around the table collecting our completed applications and forms. One by one, couples rose from the table to approach and hug and chortle over finally feeling the warm of the child in their arms. Your mother and I were last.

* * *

And now, many hours later, you are in fresh clothes. You have taken a bath and are smelling so baby-wonderful. You are sleeping alongside our bed, light breaths. You've had a whole bottle of milk, drinking wonderfully hungry, but by no means famished. You don't cry. You've smiled at us repeatedly. We feel exhausted but reunited at last—not united, but reunited. We feel you a part of us, already. So complete. So whole. Sleep dear child, sleep. We have a long journey yet ahead of us...

* * *

Today is our first full day with this new marvel in our lives. You grow in this atmosphere of abundant love the way a plant will lean toward the room's only window. We gasp at the radiant beauty of this little child, this tremulous wonder who has accepted us so immediately—and we you, of course! You woke twice in the night, having gone to bed at eight thirty; first, at eleven thirty—exactly three hours to the minute after we put you down; after a twenty minute feed you went down just before midnight, and rose at *exactly* a few minutes before three; needless to say we think you were kept on a three hour feeding schedule at the orphanage. We added some rice cereal to your formula and you slept until eight-fifteen, about four hours, after that long middle of the night feeding where you wanted to play for a while.

You are just a joy, such a "perfect" baby; no crying, except when hungry, no fuss. Just like your older sister was! We are *so* lucky! We have already won many, many smiles from you—our hearts do little butterfly beats at seeing this—and even a few heartfelt laughs when we tickle you or nibble on your middle. We each learn more about the other with every passing minute.

* * *

Following a quick Chinese breakfast of noodles, tea and cookies, we elected not to go with our group to the department store (we all need to buy things that have either run out or weren't expected—it's *far* colder here in Kunming than we ever would have guessed) and so we walked, Marcelle carrying you, Storey, (I carried a backpack with supplies!) through the Kunming streets toward our final destination: of all things, a Wal-Mart. Yes, you read that right. A Wal-Mart. Talk about oxymorons! It doesn't fit in, which is great, because if it did we would have to leave here immediately. We walked along streets lined with tiny shops, women and men on low wooden stools, all of them gaggling over you, bundled at your mother's chest, a colorful handkerchief tied around your head to keep in the warmth (we were trying to buy you a knit cap, but they don't sell them anywhere, so a kerchief it is). We saw wooden elephants and tigers for sale, jade, old hand embroidered fabric and clothing. We stopped in a roadside store and bought you a yellow and white baby outfit.

You look up or over at us, and you say thank you with those eyes; thank you for the walk in the street — I had never taken one...

Being Chinese, it has the slit trousers (Chinese kids don't wear diapers, they squat and do their business through this slit). We bought little blue shoes and some angora wool socks. We paid $7 US dollars for everything.

We stopped at crowded crosswalks in this bustling city, Chinese crowding around us, smiling, loving your beautiful face and even, I think, the fact that you were in the arms of Anglos. We were stared at, grinned at, talked to, and grabbed hold of throughout the half hour walk. We missed our mark—your father was navigator, and doing a poor job—and so I asked directions repeatedly (pointing to Chinese characters on a map I was carrying) and alas, we worked past bike shops, camera shops, noodle shops, thousands upon thousands upon thousands of pedestrians and cars and bikes streaming past in a parade of color and humanity. We reached Wal-Mart—established that there were no knit hats, no sweaters, but plenty of baby formula (you're eating so well we were afraid we might run out by the end of the week!) —and fed up with America's long arm, we headed back to the hotel by cab. We've just finished lunch, fed you a long, glorious series of bottles, and you've gone down for your nap (at 2pm, with only a brief 30 minute nap throughout the excitement of morning). We expect you will sleep a long time this afternoon—you have that look in your eyes.

Your mother is on the bed next to the crib reading; I am at the room's only desk writing you this, ready to work in a minute or two; from out the window comes the steady slow, slow drumming of some kind of machine that sounds like something huge is being pounded into the ground, the dull rhythm of it calming and soothing, as I imagine are the pats on your back. As we ate lunch today, you sat in my lap for forty-five minutes or more. I ate with chopsticks over your head, and spent much of the meal gently tapping your back as I helped you to sit in my lap. You never complained. Only sat there, cooing, smiling, chewing on your fingers, looking all around with that wide-eyed curiosity that is so intense within you. I feel the flower of your soul awakening with every minute, every image you absorb. You drink it all in, always generous enough to offer your mother or me an expression that pulls us to tears, for it is thanks. I cannot explain that look in any other way: it is gratitude. You look up or over at us, and you say thank you with those eyes; thank you for the walk in the street—I had never taken one; thank you for the taxi ride—I'd never been in one; thank you for the little hat made out of your handkerchief. You offer that look and you touch us so deeply inside. You make this all so worth it; you give so much back already. Thank you, dear girl, for the lessons you have taught us so quickly: you have made this such a special event in our lives, have rewarded us in so many glorious ways. We cannot imagine what the days ahead have in store, but we are ¾ of a family now—already this is so profound inside us—and from here there are only more such experiences, more such moments. From here there is nothing but the future. And it suddenly looks brighter than ever before.

We are settling into a routine but are almost desperately wishing we were home—not out of any desire to leave this unusual and fascinating country, but to "get on with it"—to start our family life by joining Paige whom we miss *so much* and settling in. But it is not to be: the paperwork never ends.

* * *

Today Marcelle joined the group and paid a visit to the orphanage—a complete tour of the facility—into the dorms where infants are in small cribs, one after the other. Clean but not heated, the infants bundled against the slight chill in the summer air of the high plateau. She was surprised to see so many older children, some handicapped—one such child of six or eight years stretched out his arms and appealed for an embrace, as if offering himself: "take me... take me..." She forgot the camera, but I don't think she'll lose the images any time soon.

You and I stayed behind at the hotel so you could nap. Did I mention your sleeping "routine?" Well...did *that* ever change by the second night!! You slipped quickly into a feed-me-whenever-possible mode. This translated to every two hours: a ten minute feeding; sleep for an hour and ¾ and then awake to feed again. I sleep by the crib—and I stretched the 5:30 am feeding to 7 by patting you every time you so much as twitched.

You had a great morning nap today, but we cut the afternoon nap short for a visit to the "bird and flower" market—an open air market with vendors in tiny cubicles selling everything from hamsters to wooden elephants, jade bracelets to taxidermied butterflies, Chinese pancakes to marble urns. So much color, life-chiseled faces, broken-tooth grins and women with rich black hair to their waists. Marcelle bore you in a carrier on her chest; I manned the video camera shooting stills. (Our film camera broke in a fall the first day we were here!) You drank in every face, every item, as curious and excited as your two enthralled parents.

Life spills out onto the streets here—grass grows from the tiled roofs—"minority women" in their native mountain tribe garb, bright yellows, shocking orange—and always those grins. wide-eyed and as fascinated with us as we with them. Enchanting!

Storey, you are so quickly a part of our lives! You are more beautiful with each passing moment.

My nap-sitting time included more paperwork. While at the orphanage Marcelle paid all those fresh $100 bills to cover the cost of the adoption from the orphanage itself. We inch our way closer to the visas, passports and notaries required to bring you home. Immersed in these dreaded forms, those inches can feel like miles.

You and I spent some time on a lobby couch while the room was serviced. We were approached by a Brit named Mike, and he and I discussed the Chinese economy, its politics and its people. He's been here for over a decade as an engineer for Hilton which manages more and more hotel properties here in China. This one, the Greenlake, since August 1st. Mike's job is to keep it structurally sound (we're in favor of this!). I learned so much about the inner-workings here—fascinating stuff! Kunming, host of a *huge* international horticultural expo (that's going on right now) spent $10 billion (US$) for a face-lift to look good for foreign tourists. The problem is, that's ten *years* of their annual budget. The place looks great for the next few weeks—but for nine more years they will have virtually no money for infrastructure. Thus goes the thinking here: anything to save face. The next decade be damned! Today, we look great!

Storey, you are so quickly a part of our lives! You are more beautiful with each passing moment. We tear-up watching you sleep so peacefully. We hug and count our many blessings. You make us feel so complete—I have a feeling we've been waiting for you far longer than just twenty months. We feel whole and with great purpose—and we are *so anxious* to connect with Paige and complete the circle. In the meantime, sleep precious baby, sleep.

We look forward to our phone calls—Wendy, yesterday; Betsy; L'Anne today, who told stories of Paige that made us laugh and cry. Stories everywhere. But just the one Storey here. And oh, what a story it has turned out to be! Tomorrow, a minority village (hill tribe). The adventure continues...

* * *

Picture a neglected flower drooping from its exposure to the sun, that withered leaf look, far from dead, but all its energy lost, its purpose sagging and flagging. You did not arrive that way, but you have responded as might that flower. In just two short days here we have witnessed the awe-inspiring power of love and attention. Storey, you little butterball—no shortage of food at the orphanage!—you have responded to our care in ways, and at speeds, that any parent would never believe possible. It gives me chills.

When you arrived in our arms you were bright-eyed and healthy, but little else. You could not sit up, could not lift your head, and had little hand-eye coordination. Yesterday, in my lap, while I was having a conversation with the Brit in the lobby, you sat forward from a leaning back position. All at once, and without warning. By days end, you had "sat up" (albeit from a short angle) over four times. Then, last night, only your second night in our care, you lifted your head for the first time and moved it to the other side. You astound us with how quickly you accomplish these things! How can it have been just two days? Is it possible? Twice, while in the baby carrier, you have reached out and grabbed hold of the teething ring without us noticing. But when we looked down, there you were holding the ring and grinning at us—always smiling, and laughing—big and heartfelt. We feel the joy in you, busting out like sunshine—your sweet little noises, your sparkling eyes, the way you love to touch your toes to the opposite foot and just watch them dance there. In the warmth of love (and lots of rest and plenty of food) you seem to be jumping ahead, one milestone after another, only hours apart. You have spent the day studying your hands and the entwined fingers and giggling at yourself—you are so *pleased* with everything. And it rubs off. Marcelle and I grin, teary-eyed at each other, kiss your head, coo into your ear, and watch you beam back a smile that could power a city it is so bright. To witness this effect of nurturing is an education all in itself, for the absolute power of that love reflected in you and coming back to us is so vividly clear when viewed in such a narrow time capsule. We had heard that you would excel and quickly catch up to other children—but we never expected "instant" gains like this. You amaze us at every turn. We are indebted to you for the lessons you are giving us. If this is the power of love, then why do we all reserve it for so few?

* * *

With a palatable muzak playing over the hotel room's "radio" (canned music), and with you snuggled into your crib, I sit down to write about another day in China. Your progress continues. You now hold your head up independently, and not just for a second or two—you throw your head back and forth in bed, rubbing your nose, secretly proud of this newfound ability. Showing off. Your arms are gaining strength; you can push yourself left and right in your crib, and do so freely now. Unthinkable just three days ago. You "stand" in our laps—able to support your weight—and you smile a smile as long as the Golden Gate bridge.

We are indebted to you for the lessons you are giving us. If this is the power of love, then why do we all reserve it for so few?

You "chat" —delightful baby sounds that you wouldn't share the other day. And today, for the first time, you awakened in the morning without the desperate, fingers-on-blackboard screaming you've been doing (and still do after your naps).

One wrinkle: yesterday and today, late afternoon, you have given yourself to cry and complain (very loudly) for about 90 minutes. You drink your bottle, we change your diapers, we hold you, rock you, dance with you—and still you scream. We're hoping tomorrow might bring a change—it's a difficult time of day for us, and we seem to sag a little just before dinner following this tirade.

China parades past as a stream of color and mass of humanity. Bicycles blur endlessly—more bicycles here than in the whole world combined—taxis churn. Tour buses cough down the streets. This place cooks—it rocks—morning to night. Humankind is too ever-present to allow it even a moment's rest.

We went out to dinner tonight for the first time: another hotel across town. The town is *busier* at night than in the day. We had *no idea* of this, being that we've been hitting the hay about nine every night, to keep up with the many feedings in the wee hours. But there is Kunming—bumper to bumper. Sidewalks teeming. *So many people.*

And here, we are center of attraction, even at the International Expo that owns this town right now. We went yesterday, took it in. And we became the central exhibit. Chinese by the dozen were stopping us to have their pictures taken with the tall, blond Americans and the Chinese baby. Again today at the minority village—a somewhat cheesy attempt to duplicate what and where the hill tribes live—we, all of us in the adoption group, became the targets of the Kodaks. We will be on kitchen walls from Beijing to Guilin. The Pearsons: a freak show.

Rain today. Doesn't stop anything. Guys out on the roof next door still breaking rocks with hammer and chisel; I have no idea what they're doing up there. I've been watching them for days. There's nothing to build up there: it's a flat roof of a funky three or four story building. But there are eight or nine guys out there busting up rocks every day, all day. Place looks like it'll crack under the weight.

We are beginning to gain a "locals" eye. We've been here just long enough to notice the old, old "Tudor" and brick buildings—ramshackle but stunning. Two story. Grass growing *tall* and *thick* off the ancient tile roofs. Wedged between ugly newcomers erected by a government always behind, always desperate to catch up. They never will, of course. You can't catch up with a billion people. That's a race you'll lose every time.

The Chinese are bright, inventive and, now that the economy has opened up (which it has throughout the country, though this is not widely publicized), creative entrepreneurs. Capitalism is a many-headed dragon here. It is devouring the government's attempts to be what it once was. There are Chinese here in Kunming who speak three languages and have not yet been to Beijing, but have been to Las Vegas *twice*. There are Lexus cars in the streets (in a country with 100% import tax on luxury vehicles). *It is cooking* here. You feel it. It's inescapable. And when this economy finally busts loose of the lame attempts to contain it, as it most certainly must—and soon, no doubt—the world is in for a shock. Labor in this country is dirt cheap—absurdly cheap, embarrassingly cheap. When that labor force becomes more trained, more educated, even more hungry for what the west has to offer.... *look out*. It's going to blow the doors off anything we've ever seen. Tsunami, here we come....

We are loving it here, but *so* anxious to get home. As a group we are restless. We await paperwork. Patience is running thin. The group itself is disjointed and not feeling like a team, but instead a group of disparate players. Marcelle and I live for the morning phone calls and the emails from family and friends. We are isolated here—in a hotel room that is constantly too cold, in a country where we are the favorite freak show, and with our other daughter home waiting for us. Tuesday we finally head to Guangzhou and the last leg of this amazing journey. And none too soon. Were we simple tourists, we would be in hog heaven; but we're new parents, a partial family awaiting permissions and stamps and notarizations, and our focus remains getting out of here, safe, sound and intact.

Despite all of this, each day is invigorating, exciting and leaves us filled with wonder. The Chinese people are so wonderful. Huge smiles everywhere we go (and those cameras) —hard, hard workers, and eternal optimists. We have no idea what tomorrow holds for us, but we're eager to find out.

* * *

These last few days, all spent in Guangzhou (old Canton), a city of six million that should be about 2 million, have been a whirlwind of medical appointments, photos, and panic attacks. In the few remaining hours, we did manage to get into the streets of the old city and wander an enormous neighborhood, endless really, of open air markets and tiny shops, one after the other. The atmosphere is more SciFi than reality, apartments stacked on top of apartments, laundry high overhead, chickens and turtles and eels out for sale, the pungent smells that turn one's head, the thick smog and thicker humidity. A landscape of human on top of human. Curio and tea shops selling over fifty varieties of Chinese medicinal teas. We encountered a young man named Billy, and anyone who has seen Year of Living Dangerously knows the significance of that name. Just like in the film, Billy escorted us deeper and deeper into the urban outback, in search of antiques (my eyes wide open so we wouldn't be burned)—and down a narrow lane where we sat with a woman and negotiated over two Ming Dynasty rice bowls for the better part of thirty minutes—Marcelle and I sweating from the unbelievable heat and sipping from sodas we had bought on the street—Sprite and Orange with straws delivered by tweezers to prove the vendor had not touched them.

We stepped back in time, the heat sucking us down, the woman negotiating with us through our little Billy and his clipped English. In the end we didn't buy, but OH what an experience. We shall never forget it. And you in the cuddly at Marcelle's chest, eyes wide, curiosity never ceasing. What a jewel you are. What a mystery.

* * *

By last night we had seemingly satisfied the last of our requirements—a medical exam where the women doctors were truly kind and gentle to the babies—and more and more paperwork. Marcelle attended a late night hallway meeting (this hotel has floor hostesses who memorize each guest and point you to your room as you come out of the elevator). Panic was in the air. The American Consulate had found problems with our papers (everyone's) and were warning that our adoptions would be denied.

You can't imagine how it felt to have come so very far—so many days, miles and agonies—to hear this news. One member from each family was dispatched to the Consulate at 9pm to argue our case. I stayed behind to deal with you, my fussy child—Marcelle and others walked down the street to the Consulate and attempted to rectify the situation, only to infuriate a woman delegate who had to come downtown at that time of night. It went horribly bad.

By eleven o'clock I was on the computer writing a note to plead for a couple of our dear friends to use their pull with the Consular General and attempt to put out this fire. At midnight, the email ready, I called Lin, our adoption agent here, and she requested I not send the plea. She had one last trick up her sleeve: fly another agent from Kunming with new, notarized documents in a midnight-hour desperation attempt to resolve the issue. But first, she wanted to see how our final interviews at the Consulate went.

* * *

At 8:30 this morning we gathered in the hotel and reviewed all our paperwork individually—we knew the Consulate would be gunning for us now, because we had angered them the night before—we wanted every T crossed, every I dotted.

Our days in China draw to a close with the first unbroken blue sky since our arrival.

With paperwork prepared, at 9:40 we headed off en mass to the Consulate for our tightly scheduled adoption interviews—the penultimate event in legalizing our children. Only the actual delivery of the visa would follow, if all went well, late afternoon the next day.

We entered a room about 500 square feet, and about 55 degrees—air conditioning set to keep the room cool over the next six to eight hours as bodies warmed it one by one. We were freezing! They were angry at us. Lin got chewed out by an assistant director and was in tears. Things did not look good. Within three quarters of an hour there were forty of us in the room—forty!—babies everywhere, nervous parents, and two Chinese to check paperwork and two Americans to do the interview—all in the open, all in the same room. Time stopped. Thirty minutes passed. An hour. An hour and a half. The Pearsons were called. We went through our *huge* stack of paperwork with the Chinese assistants. We passed muster. Go sit on the couch and wait for your interview. What couch? Another ten people and their babies had entered the room. It looked like a frat party phone booth. A madhouse. Kids everywhere. Tension you could cut with a knife. Lin announced that she thought they would accept the paperwork being flown in by hand from Kunming. Time dragged out. We were the *last* of our group to sit for our interview. The man was incredibly nice (said my name sounded familiar to him, "What do you write?"—we're sending him a hardback. We spoke for only minutes; he apologized for all the politics and tears and refusals.

We lifted our right arms, a knot in our throats, tears trying for our eyes one final time, and we swore to the United States government that we would protect and cherish this little wonder for the rest of our lives. We married you, little Storey. We said "I do," and our hands went down and we were a family.

This is another of those moments I shall not lose. Not ever. "I do." The man's red hair, his suspenders. The noise in that cold room. "I do." Little Storey in our lives forever now. A member of the

Pearson family. Little Storey, quiet and still wide-eyed: fascinated we would bother with a man with red hair.

We stood and we walked out of that place, back into the oppressive heat of Guangzhou, down a peaceful street under a row of Banyan trees, the three of us, walking close together, kissing, leaning against each other. You looking up into our faces. You do this all the time: just look and stare. "You're still here…" your dark eyes seem to say. "You're still here…"

And now we're here forever, Little One. We have the passport—the visa arrives at the hotel tomorrow, God willing. We have airline reservations. We have hope. In our hearts. On our faces. In our smiles. In your loving eyes. Hope. It's why we came here; and with it now firmly entrenched in us, we leave. Out of Guangzhou, bound for home.

Home and hope. We hum those words, and they mean more to us than ever before.

* * *

Our days in China draw to a close with the first unbroken blue sky since our arrival. Gray haze hangs over Guangzhou like a noose—this air will choke this city to death someday. The sampans, Chinese barges and freighters steam up and down the Pearl River loaded with everything imaginable, especially sand—bound for cement companies, no doubt, or glass smelters, for this is a country quickly made of concrete and glass, all other raw materials long since consumed. There is an article in the newspaper, edited by the communists, that mentions China's population as 22% of the world's human count; by contrast they have 10% of farmable earth on the planet. They see a small conflict in those numbers, and are quickly pouring money into irrigation projects to increase their food output. They are the New York Giants of developing countries: defense, defense, deeeeefense. All the articles are cast in this mold: "in order to protect our emerging socialist economy," "in order to protect our people," —the plowshares that made the guns of fifty years earlier are coming back as plowshares. Too many mouths. Too many mouths.

But on the street there is a churning energy of get-it-done. Infectious. Attractive. We would come back here to live for a few months if given the chance. It's the same fascination with an ant farm as a youngster: How do they *do* that? We watch. Intrigued. Numbed.

And we smile. At three-thirty on this day, the 3rd of September, 1999, we received your entry visa into the US. We have that paper in hand. We can go home. You are not only a member of our family, but a guest of the United States until we can effect your citizenship—about 18 more months, if the stories are true.

The tension is still in our necks, still creeps into our voices at odd times. We've been living right on, right against the knife blade, and we have the emotional scars to prove it. Thanks to our friends and our faith, we—the three of us—have endured. I had a chop made—a stone stamp for signing my contracts. On it is my business logo (my initials with the R backward) and beneath this, the Chinese characters for prosperity. That is what we take away from here: one small bundle of human being and the hope of prosperity for a family now awakening.

Paige, who is with us in our thoughts each minute, and on the phone each morning here, pulls us toward home like a satellite toward earth: we stretch to reach there all the sooner.

We leave behind tears and trials, terror and joy. We bring home God's greatest gift of all: a human bundle of pure and perfect love. We leave behind thousands more like you. I've dreamt of these children at night, haunted by the thought of the others left behind and the futile knowledge that they only escape one at a time.

The other day in the thick and congested open air market, we turned down a narrow lane to noise and a large gathering of Chinese, all pressed up one against the other. Wondering what could attract people so...a dignitary? a calamity?...we approached somewhat cautiously. Why all the noise, all the keen stares toward the gated building? We finally found ourselves swallowed by the throng, for it closed in around us as the gate opened. And there was our answer: children. It was a school. The students, about ten to twelve years old, were being let out of school one child at a time, the eager parent waiting outside as if this child had come home from war. As if this child were the only child on earth...and of course they are. One family, one child. For nearly twenty years now. These are the rarest of all assets, the harbingers of China's future— one precious child, greeted each day after school like a returning veteran.

And at the White Swan Hotel, twenty, thirty, perhaps fifty or more such children checking out each day and boarding buses for the airport in the arms of their American, German, or Canadian parents. One family, one child. And in rare cases, twins. Ten. Twenty. Thirty. Each day. Every day. An adoption factory at full throttle. Yet only skimming surface of those we leave behind.

And one of those couples will be smiling quite brightly tomorrow at noon as they pass through those doors. A little glimpse of a miracle. A magical moment. You still study everything around you with that innate curiosity of a young baby, but you stare at the two of us equally hard, for an equally long time. You stare and stare, and grin every now and then, grin up into our returning gaze with wonder and excitement in your eyes. And the world stops for that moment. No one is aware of it—people think their lives go on as they do every day—but the whole world stops for that blink of an eye, and three people in a cab on the back streets of Guangzhou hold their breaths and make sure this is real. And it is. Which for them makes it the greatest story of all....

— *Ridley Pearson*

Paige, Ridley, and Storey
photo courtesy of Ridley Pearson

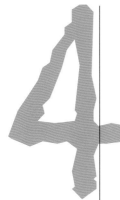

Family Building From Foster Care

We lived in a garage. My mom and dad would leave me alone, frequently, with my two younger sisters and at a young age I learned to be a parent. I would even bring home snacks from school to feed my sisters, because they were hungry.

The Bible speaks of a man, in Luke, who falls among robbers: "They stripped him of his clothes, beat him and went away, leaving him half dead."

I too, was stripped and beaten: stripped of my youth and beaten down emotionally. I too, was dying inside.

The Bible tells how many people, including a Priest and Levite, walked passed the beaten man offering no assistance. I, too, understand that kind of pain. Many people, including close relatives, neighbors and friends of my parents', turned their heads and did nothing to help three neglected little girls.

For the beaten man in Luke 10, a Good Samaritan finally arrived: "He bandaged his wounds, pouring on oil and wine. Then he put the man on his own donkey, took him to an inn and took care of him."

I believe in Good Samaritans. For my sisters and me, they came in the form of Social Services and a family I had never met.

A social worker took my sisters and me away from my parents. She asked me many questions: she said, "one or two?" I didn't know what she meant but I answered, "two."

I came to understand that 'one' meant I would be going to a foster family without my sisters, and 'two' meant that one of my sisters would go with me. I worried about my youngest sister, as I would no longer be there to make sure she ate, or to hug her when she missed us.

I was now a foster child. We were now foster children. Like the beaten man in the Bible, our wounds were being bandaged and we slowly began to heal as our foster families cared for our needs.

As time moved on, I began having visits with my mom and dad. Those visits brought with them many mixed feelings. I felt pain and sadness, but mostly anger as I searched for answers to questions like: Why didn't they take care of my sisters and me? Why did we live in a garage and not in a house? Why did all of these bad things happen to us? Had we done something wrong? I came to understand that my parents felt they had better things to do than to care for their own children.

Ten months after being in my first foster home, my sisters and I were finally placed together under the same roof. Like the beaten man in the Bible who was taken to an inn and cared for, this new foster home became our inn: the place where my life truly began. This is the place where I learned the real meaning of family. This is the place where I received the mercy I had been crying out for.

On December 21, 1997 this foster family became our forever family, as my sisters and I were adopted.

I am thirteen years old now and I love my life. I have five sisters, a great mom and dad, and so many wonderful friends: all of the things I knew that, at age 6, I was supposed to have.

—*Anonymous Author*

Love at First Sight

Len

I walked into the library to meet my friend who is a licensed foster parent. She normally brings children with her on Tuesdays, as story hour is a scheduled event. I walked over to the children's section and saw her sitting at a small table with the cutest little boy I had ever seen. She said his name was Len and introduced me to him. I said hello to Len and he looked up at me and smiled, replying with a simple, "Hi." My heart was, at once, lost to this little guy.

My friend told me that Len, soon to be five-years old, had been bounced around from foster home to foster home and that this instability had taken its toll on him. He had severe temper tantrums, along with bouts of acting out that were sometimes uncontrollable. I listened as my friend commented that Len would soon be available for adoption.

I ran home and called my husband at work, asking, "What would you think about adopting a five-year old boy?" He said he would have to think about it. We already had two children, a 24-year old son who lives away from home and a 20-year old daughter in college. We were 'empty-nesters' now. Still, on the phone, I added, "You will have to meet him before you can make a decision." My husband agreed and we arranged a meeting through Len's foster mother.

My husband's heart was also touched at this first meeting. We decided to move forward and get Len into our home. We prepared ourselves and passed all of the necessary requirements to begin our life with Len. Challenges began shortly after Len came into our home. His behavior was out of control. He was an angry little boy and had every right to be. He physically attacked me. He would destroy things in his room. I felt helpless. I could see that Len was very bright and that his speech delay and emotional trouble were due to being bounced around and not belonging in any one place.

My husband and I had Len tested and he was diagnosed with ADHD* (Attention Deficit Hyperactivity Disorder). Len started behavior therapy. There were nights I would cry myself to sleep and wonder if I was doing the right thing.

Nevertheless, my husband and I both were determined to work through Len's anger and hurt, and all the trials ADHD can bring. After three months, we began to see progress. Through love and consistent behavior modification we started to see a breakthrough. We would tell Len, "No matter what you do or say, we will never send you away. We love you and we want you to be our little boy." He was so happy to be getting a mom and dad. He was so happy to be able to stay in one home and not have to go anywhere else again.

On December 18, 2001 Len became our son, legally. He is a blessing to our family. His older brother and sister adore him and his grandma spoils him. Len does well in school and is a math star in the first grade. His behavior is not a problem any longer. He is a happy seven-year old with a mom and dad, a family, and a home he can call his own. We never once wanted to give up on him and we have been rewarded with a wonderful son.

Is it worth it? Most definitely! Would we do it all over again? Absolutely!

—*Kit Moody,* Florida
*A definition of ADHD can be found in the Glossary of Terms.

Unconditional Love

Herman, Andrew, John, Ashanti, Danny, Aramis, Eric & Darren

Adoption has been a significant part of my family now for three generations. I had always expected that one day I would adopt one or two kids of my own, but never expected to adopt seven kids before being married. And in my wildest dreams, I could have never imagined that I would one day be sitting in the White House listening to the President of the United States praise our family in a speech. But that's exactly where my boys and I found ourselves on December 2, 2003, when President Bush delivered a speech on the Adoption Promotion Act and afterwards, personally congratulated us on our inspiring story.

As a result of this experience and all of the positive media attention our family has been receiving over the past year, I have taken some time to reflect upon what exactly makes our story so inspiring. Clearly, the fact that all of my boys have gone from failure to success has caught a lot of people's attention. All of them came directly out of foster care and had experienced numerous rejections and failed foster placements before coming to me. Many people had given up on them and saw them as failures and troublemakers, but I saw each of them as a diamond in the rough, a hurt and wounded child, who had built up all sorts of defenses in order to survive in the system. Perception is everything, and if you're expecting trouble and problems, that's generally what you'll get. But I had different expectations of my boys and that is probably why I got different results than any of their previous foster parents had gotten. Focusing on the positive instead of the negative can dramatically alter a child's attitude and behavior.

The fact is, all of my kids did come to me with a lot of issues and baggage that I had to deal with, but I gave them the message from day one that I would not give up on them and that I would be with them for the long haul, and that seems to be what's made all of the difference for them.

Unconditional love has been a tremendously powerful tool in transforming each of their lives and giving them a sense of belonging and permanency. One by one, as each of them realized the reality of the commitment I was making to them, their attitudes and behavior began to change. They let down their guards and they began to bond with me and the rest of their new family.

Perhaps, one of the best illustrations of the power of unconditional love occurred when I met my son Danny for the first time. He was twelve years old when I went to the foster care agency to meet him. Before meeting him that day, I first had to meet with the social workers and staff, who gave me his history and an overview of some of his issues and problems. They told me that he was being treated for depression and that he was being kicked out of his current foster home because of his unmanageable behavior. One thing that was pointed out to me was that because of his difficulty trusting people and forming relationships, he would never look people in the eye when he talked to them. This fact became readily apparent to me when I was brought into the room and introduced to Danny for the first time.

As I entered the room where Danny was sitting, he was hunched over in a chair, staring at the ground. He took a quick glance at me as I entered the room, but never looked up at me again as I was introduced to him and as I pulled up a chair and sat down in front of him. I told him a little about my family and me and then began asking him some questions about himself. He answered all of my questions by either nodding or mumbling one or two-word answers that were barely audible. At one point, I said to him, "Danny, I'm not really interested in just becoming another foster parent for you. I would really like to adopt you and make you a permanent part of my family. Is that something you'd be interested in?" Without hesitating, he looked up, making perfect eye contact with me, and with a sheepish grin on his face said, "Yeah." I will remember that moment for the rest of my life.

From that point on, Danny literally never had a problem looking people in the eye again, and within a few weeks, he was taken off of his anti-depressant medication. The social workers and staff at the agency were amazed at this and kept questioning me as to what I had done to bring about such an incredible change in such a short period of time. In reality, I hadn't had much time yet to do anything significant for Danny in terms of parenting him. All I had done was offer him unconditional love and my commitment not to give up on him and that made all the difference in the world for him, transforming his life in an incredible way.

Like all of my other kids, Danny came to me with a lot of emotional and behavioral issues, but we worked through those things together and today he is a very happy and well adjusted sixteen-year old. My willingness to stick with him and not give up on him has created an incredibly strong bond between us. It has also helped him to come out of his shell and trust other people as well.

Raising seven boys alone can be very challenging, but the rewards have far outweighed the challenges. I never intended to have seven sons before being married, but sometimes God's plans are different than ours. By following His will, He has enabled me to totally change the direction of my children's lives. The blessings I've received have been abundant. The greatest of these blessings has been my wife, who joined our family earlier this year. She is not only everything I've ever dreamed of in a wife, but she is also everything my boys have always dreamed of in a mother. She will be legally adopting all seven of my sons and we are now in the process of adopting our eighth child. In some ways, our family is now complete, but in reality, we are more like a work in progress that will likely have a few more additional "chapters" before it is complete.

—*Jim Morris,* New York

H

He was a six-year old boy with freckles on his face, which assisted in making him as cute as a button.

During a counseling session, six months after he came into our lives, he was asked what his three fondest wishes were in life. He answered: "A television in my room, a trampoline, and to live with this family forever." As foster parents, we weren't 'planning' to adopt. My, oh my, how plans change!

We knew we could grant two of this little boy's three wishes, but the trampoline was just too big a request for this overprotective momma!

—*Jackie Brookins,* Alabama

Better Late Than Never

John

I've heard it said that life begins at forty, but in my case, life began at the age of fifty-six. Little did I know that after retiring from a thirty-year career in a government position, my life would change so drastically.

As a single person, I have always been involved with children in one way or another. I could often be found babysitting for the kids of my married friends, volunteering for the Big Brothers/Big Sisters organization, or mentoring a child through the Department of Children and Families (DCF).

I strongly felt that I had something to offer a child and would, someday, have one or more of my own children. That prospect looked bleak, though, as marriage eluded me.

In the spring of 1998, I attended an Open House sponsored by the Waterford Country School (WCS) in Waterford, Connecticut. I learned about the process of becoming a foster parent, but at the time felt I wasn't ready for this type of commitment. Thanks to the persistence of the Foster Care staff at WCS, I was given the opportunity to prove that I, indeed, was responsible and could commit to caring for a child, on a full-time basis.

Some people, however, need a gentle shove and in the spring of 1999, I experienced one. Waterford Country School phoned me asking if I was still interested in foster care.

In July of 1999, after completing a nine-week foster care course at WCS, with the intention of only doing volunteer work at the school, I was told that I would be a great fit within the respite care division. Respite care would require that I look after foster kids, while their caregivers are away or in need of a break. I agreed and welcomed a twelve-year-old boy into my home for three weeks. This was quite an introduction for someone who had recently retired and was getting fat and lazy. Those three weeks went by quickly and three days after he left, I was asked if I would take a nine-year old boy who could no longer stay where he was placed. I again agreed and as the days turned into weeks and then months, I realized that this wasn't respite care but honest to goodness foster care. Because this boy and I were getting along quite well, I informed the caseworkers at WCS and DCF that I would continue caring for him, for as long as it took to resolve his situation. I have to add, that all this would not be possible without the continued support and guidance of both WCS and DCF. I met with them regularly at their offices for quarterly treatment plan updates or through monthly home visits. We also met throughout the year, along with school officials, to review his progress in school. There was also a six month review involving biological parents (if applicable), the parent's and child's lawyers, therapists, and DCF personnel from headquarters in Hartford. I had no doubt regarding the total commitment these amazing professionals showed in the well being of this boy.

I, for one, can attest to the rewards received in helping a child. At my age, I might be the last person anyone would think of to be a foster parent.

If I can do it, anyone can!

No, it isn't always easy and may not be for everyone, but you won't know if you don't give it a try. At this stage in my life, having a child tell me that he loves me and feels safe with me is absolutely amazing. When my son calls me "Dad," well, words can't describe the feeling I get.

John came to live with me in July of 1999, with the intention of possible re-unification with his biological father and my efforts were directed at that goal. As it turns out, this was not to be and both biological parents terminated their rights in February of 2001. Having been John's foster father for nearly two years, I was asked if I would consider adopting him. So many questions loomed inside my brain.

Questions such as:
"Am I the right person for him?"
"Would he be better off with a two parent family?"
"I'm old enough to be his grandfather. Do I have the stamina?"

With every fearful thought, the fact that I had been caring for a wonderful little boy whose behavior had stabilized remarkably, who loves me as much as I love him and wanted me to adopt him, proved that there could only be one answer.

I'm pleased to say that John has progressed so well academically that he was able to transition from a special education school to a local school in September of 2001. I'm also pleased to say that the adoption took place on May 30, 2002 and fifty-nine-year old Dave and twelve-year old John became a forever family. We have a strong bond and love each other very much, even though John says I am a little over-protective and tell really lame jokes.

Can a child make a difference? You bet!

Foster care, and now adoption, has given me a family. God brought John to me and my first priority is to see that I help him become the best young adult he can be. John says, "It was love that brought us together and the best present a dad can give is love."

Adopting John was the best decision I ever made and I encourage everyone to consider foster care and adoption. It does keep me young, being both "mom" and dad. If you have room in your heart and room in your home, you should give it a try. John agrees and says, "The best gift you can give someone is a home. If I was an adult, I would adopt." He adds, "You are giving them hope by being part of a family."

—*David Bishop,* Connecticut

We Built It and They Came

Matthew & Isaac

On the wall of the boys' bedroom in our home, there is a quote in bright red letters that reads: "If you build it, they will come." It seemed only fitting that our favorite quote from our favorite movie, "Field of Dreams," would be proudly displayed in this sports-themed room as we prepared to welcome foster children into our lives. My husband and I had no idea that our dreams were about to be fulfilled!

After fourteen years of praying for children, we made the difficult decision to stop all infertility treatments and pursue a family by other methods. God was leading us in a direction that we had never talked about–foster care. So many children in our area were in need of safe homes and we committed ourselves to opening up our hearts to those little ones who were most in need.

A few months after making the decision to be foster parents, my husband and I received our first placements. Two little girls, ages 18 months and 7 years, came to us with emotional scars. Within months the scars began to heal and they blossomed into lovely girls who trusted us. After six months, they were returned to family members and are doing well.

Three weeks before the girls were to leave our home, we received a call from State Adoptions. We were told a three-year old boy and his thirteen-year old sister were available for adoption. My husband and I met with the siblings and felt an attraction to both of them. We purchased a new bedroom set for the little boy with a bunk bed dressed in red and blue sheets and sports memorabilia on the walls. Mike and I started dreaming of the future with children of our own.

Then came the call that wrecked that dream. An Uncle of the little boy and teenaged girl had decided to take the children. Furniture was being delivered to our house the next day and we had just found out that there would be no children to grace the room we were so lovingly decorating.

Mike and I cried for sometime in an empty room when suddenly a feeling of strength came over us. We stood on two chairs and applied our beloved quote to the walls of a room, where someday we hoped children would sleep.

"If you build it, they will come."

And they did! Two days later we received the phone call that changed our lives. A neighboring county had two little boys, ages six and two, who were in need of a home. On July 18, 2002 we walked into a local restaurant and saw the two most beautiful boys in the world waiting to meet us.

Matthew, the oldest, held no reservations and asked a million questions about his new room, his new school, and if a bike was waiting for him. Isaac, the youngest, didn't speak for some time and then, out of the blue, he blurted out, "Sponge Bob!" I looked at him and repeated, "Sponge Bob?" Isaac smiled at me with a grin that could light up any room. We had connected!

The first few days with the boys were ones of adjustment for everyone involved. For over a year, Matthew had spent every waking moment trying to protect his little brother from being abused, so we had to hurdle a huge obstacle of trust right away. My husband and I also had to prove to Isaac that we would never hurt him. My heart broke the first time I said "no" to him and he instantly went into a fetal position waiting to be beaten. I cried for hours and prayed that someday these two precious boys would heal from their traumatic past.

Social Services was working to reunite the boys with their mother and so weekly visits were scheduled to allow Matthew and Isaac to spend time with their biological family. These visits, for us, were heartbreaking as we watched the boys avoid their own mother. I struggled during these visits as we continued to learn the history of abuse the boys had endured. Matthew began weekly therapy sessions as he was diagnosed with Post Traumatic Stress Disorder. Mike and I were learning, through these sessions, how to help Matthew heal and move forward with his life.

One week before the boys' hearing in September 2002, their social worker called and said, "We are not going to send the boys home to their mother. Would you be interested in adopting them?"

I replied without hesitation – "Yes!" And then I added, "We've been praying for this moment since we first met the boys last July. Our answer is yes, we would love to adopt the boys."

Mike and I sat in a courtroom on February 28, 2003 and listened as a judge introduced us as the boys' prospective adoptive parents. We continued to listen as the judge told us that we could finalize the adoption within as little as sixty days.

The adoption actually took a few weeks longer than that to finalize, due to a shortage of caseworkers, but on June 18, 2003, exactly one year to the day they came into our home, Matthew and Isaac became our "forever boys."

Our very own field of dreams came true. Matthew and Isaac have both healed and have grown to trust us, and they've learned what it is to be loved.

As the boys run down the hallway of our home, giggling and chasing each other, I can't help but think, "we built it and they came!"

—*Stephanie Bixler,* California

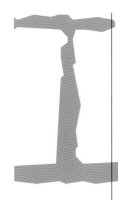

Life couldn't have been better on that sunny summer's day. I was trying out my 'new' fifteen-year old motorboat, on Lake Sunapee, with my very best childhood friend. Little did I know that my life would be turned upside down within the next five minutes.

As the warm breeze was blowing across my face, I remember having a smile that even a 20-knot wind wasn't able to wipe off. My cell phone rang and I picked it up to hear my former wife, Cindy, inform me that I needed to meet her in Massachusetts at U-Mass Medical Center, as soon as possible, but that I shouldn't worry. Many thoughts ran through my head as I traveled back to Worcester.

I followed Cindy's directions and met her on a specified floor by the nurse's station. We were immediately brought into a conference room. There a team of doctors wasted no time and directly, and very bluntly, stated to us that our eleven-year old daughter, Christina, had a very rare form of terminal cancer. They predicted she would be gone within the year. I felt as if I had been struck in the chest with a sledgehammer. My body went limp as my head hit the hard conference table.

There were many ups and downs over the next eleven months. We tried everything possible, from experimental treatments to medicine men and women. Unfortunately, all the prayers, medicines, surgeries, and treatments ended abruptly. At about 5:00 A.M., eleven months after that terrible meeting, my then twelve-year old daughter said the angels were coming to get her. She went with them as her body went limp.

Words cannot explain what this does to a parent. Often, I still believe I'm in the middle of a nightmare. Soon I will wake up and it will all be over.

My current wife Mary, although a great stepmom, had always insisted that she was a career person and not the mothering type. About six months after Christina's death, we saw an advertisement in our local paper, seeking prospective foster and adoptive parents. We attended the training and within a year, we were licensed foster parents. We had a nice home and plenty of toys and love to give.

Life is funny sometimes. Mary had an accident on the job and became permanently disabled. She could not continue the career she had always known, but I'm happy to report she has a great new career now. Mary is a Super Mom. I left the corporate world and became a teacher at the age of forty-five.

Over the years, we have had a host of foster kids and are particularly blessed to have adopted two wonderful and loving children. Our daughter is now fourteen and our son is eight. Mary is very active in the New Hampshire Foster and Adoptive Parent Association. Who would have thought this was our calling? It may sound strange to you, but I feel Christina has had a hand in all of this.

When I ask myself why I became a foster and adoptive parent, with all the trials and tribulations often associated with this challenging but rewarding lifestyle, my answer is clear. Eight years after Christina's death, her legacy lives on within me. . . guiding me. She will live in my heart and soul for the rest of my days.

—Mark Richmond, New Hampshire

Author's Note: Christina wrote a book before she passed away entitled, *Chemo Girl.* Her story helps other children get through tough and often painful Chemotherapy and Radiation treatments. Her life is a testimony of strength and endurance, so often found within the experiences of children in foster care. I believe that this is where the link can be discovered. Adoption Means Love (The AML Foundation) and Adoption Tribe Publishing honor Christina: her life and her legacy. We thank her beautiful spirit for guiding Mark and Mary.

—MMB

Balloons of Hope

Natalie

I remember the night police officers knocked on the door of my birth parents' home. The year was 1984. My birthmother ran around the house in a panic as she tried to hide drug paraphernalia.

I was five years of age and the oldest of my siblings. That night we were removed from our house and taken directly to the local hospital for physical exams. Although I felt scared and sad, the nurses were kind as they gave us popcorn and coloring books. Upon leaving the hospital, we were taken into the custody of Social Services.

I wanted to cry as we were checked into the child shelter, but I knew I had to be strong for my younger siblings. I told my brothers, Rudy and Alfredo, not to eat the food or do as staff members asked. I was rebelling, hoping they would send us back home. I soon found out we would not be returning to our former lives.

The next day, we were moved from the shelter into foster homes. My brothers were placed in the same home, while I went to a different one. I remember feeling a wide range of emotions from sadness to fear. Mostly, however, I was worried. I was the parental figure to my younger brothers and sister and felt a deep sense of sorrow upon our separation.

I stayed in my first foster home for a little over a year. I was moved to a different home due to prejudices over my ethnicity. In December of 1986, I was taken to yet another new foster home. At the time, I was unaware that this would be the place where I would find Lanise Hines: my forever mother.

I remember the first day I met Lanise. She was single and shared her home with her very cute dog, "Smidgen." My social worker took me to meet my new mom and I was nervous and shy as we toured my new room.

When I was placed with Lanise, I was a child with low self-esteem. I had not been taught morals or values and had no hopes or dreams. That, however, would change. I was adopted on June 3, 1988: my eighth birthday!

It seems my adoption created an awakening inside. I remember walking into the courthouse, on that special day, with my mom. We were both wearing new dresses. I felt happy and had butterflies in my stomach. The judge smiled at me and asked, "Would you like Lanise to be your mom forever?" I replied, "Yes!"

After the adoption, I went back to class and ironically, my school was holding a special event where students wrote letters and attached them to balloons for release. Even though I knew this was an annual affair, I felt special because I believed the balloons were for me, in honor of my special day. They were my balloons of hope.

My outlook on life has changed over the years due to tons of effort, patience, and dedication shown by my mom. The belief I have in myself has soared. Achieving straight A's in school, graduating tenth in my class, and earning twelve different scholarships are just some of my achievements.

Once a shy little girl, I have now blossomed into a confident young woman involved in clubs and sports. I have discovered an amazing musical talent within and the ability to succeed in life.

I was brought up in a loving and caring environment with people who believe in me and support me. The blessings of adoption have influenced my personality and my career decision. I have been inspired to become a social worker focusing on adoptions. It is my dream that I can help other children discover their balloons of hope.

—*Natalie F. Coronado,* Colorado

Jeremiah Was a Bullfrog

We were brand new foster parents when the Department of Social Services called us to take in a very special boy. Jeremiah was a youngster with many special needs and there was some concern over whether we possessed the skills to deal with them. We agreed to foster him, with the stipulation that the department would understand if we felt him too challenging for our home.

Jeremiah was ten-years old when he came to us and wore size 4T clothing. He was tiny but made up for his small physical appearance with a large personality. We were told that Jeremiah was mentally challenged. He was still able to remember dates and helped me keep track of the many scheduled medical appointments. So often, he argued with me over which doctor we would be seeing on a particular day.

He's a character, indeed! Jeremiah kept us laughing all of the time. One of our favorite foster care stories about him goes something like this: Jeremiah threw a tantrum one day (a common occurrence) and I sent him to his room for some quiet time. When he came back, he sat down at the table and put his head in his hands. I said, "Jeremiah, you look like you are still mad." He replied, "I am going to run away." I asked him where he was going to go. He grumbled, "To the moon." With a slight smile and a twinkle in my eye, I asked, "How are you going to get there?" Jeremiah looked me straight in the eye and answered, "I'm gonna borrow your broom!"

Still laughing, I questioned the mentally challenged diagnosis given to Jeremiah. This little boy was quick!

Jeremiah remained with us for two years and then was adopted into a terrific family. We learned a great deal from Jeremiah and hope we gave him something in return. I'm sure he gives his family as much laughter as he gave us. He is a blessing.

—Joyce Pringle, Maine

Coffee Anyone?

When my second oldest son, who happens to be one of my biological children, was about thirteen years old, our family attended a state foster and adoptive conference. There were approximately one hundred children, of all ages, running around. My son teamed up wih two boys of his own age.

As these boys were talking and getting to know one another, one of the boys said, "I am adopted." The other kid said, "I am foster." The two boys then looked at my son and asked, "What are you?" My son quickly answered, "I am regular."

—Johnna Breland, Alabama

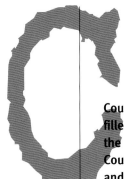

A "Rae" of Sunshine
Courtney Rae

Courtney Rae arrived at my home clutching a bag filled with toys and clothes. Her eyes darted around the room as she took in her new surroundings. Courtney Rae looked at her relinquishing foster mother and then focused her eyes on me, her new foster/pre-adoption mother. Standing firm, she angrily declared, "I hate you. You stink and this house stinks too!"

Our first night together was consumed with a little girl's rage as Rae kicked the walls and screamed, "I don't have any mama!" Exhausted and drenched in perspiration, she finally fell asleep. It was at this point that I approached her and began stroking her head and touching her fingers and toes, in awe. I fought back tears of sorrow as she, even in a deep sleep, clutched her jaw and tightened her face.

Courtney Rae looked so much older than her seven years and my joy of welcoming her into my life was dampened only by the realization that this child's losses were huge. Her pain evoked memories of my own lengthy experience in foster care, many years earlier. From that personal knowledge, I knew that on this night a part of Courtney Rae's spirit had died. I sat watching her sleep and I wondered if she had enough strength left to heal.

Over the following weeks, Courtney Rae, struggled to gain control over her losses and would often declare, "I am the boss!" She was inconsistent in accepting kind gestures, loving touch, or comfort of any type. One night, she impishly complained, "Lady, you forgot to hug me goodnight." Encouraged and hopeful, I quickly went to her side only to have her smack my hand away. For me, this was a positive sign of the strength I had been praying to find Rae was open and receptive to being loved, even if she still felt conflicted and distrusting.

Courtney Rae's desire to please others made her easy to motivate. From the beginning, she was very responsible with chores. She began mothering a stray kitten I brought home and relayed her personal story through this tiny animal. Sometimes she asked about the kitten's 'real' mother and 'real' home.

Still, her anger surfaced at unexpected moments and her sleep patterns were disrupted. At night, she would hide under my bed and I would awaken to find her asleep on the floor. Courtney Rae was overweight and highly dependent on food for comfort. At times she ate with her hands or put her face in a plate and gulped down bites, with no self-consciousness.

Yet, Courtney Rae did especially well in parochial school as she was curious about everything and displayed strong academic skills. Her teacher and principal felt that Courtney Rae's potential was enormous and praised her for her excellent reading and math abilities. Rae was eager to prepare for Baptism and First Communion. She volunteered to be an altar girl at church and within a short time was 'adopted' by our church family.

Courtney Rae and I found recreation to be our main source of bonding. We camped in the woods or slept in sleeping bags on the trampoline in our back yard. Jumping rope, swimming and playing hide and seek were regular activities. She joined the Brownies and I volunteered with Habitat for Humanity. We cooked together, spent hours with friends, played dolls and worked out compromises with music and movies.

Courtney Rae's daily actions began to show greater signs of hope. She asked, "When I grow up can I have a key to your house so I can come see you?" Within months, she began to speak of growing up with me and revealed her plans for our future together. However, that future was still uncertain. Courtney Rae had been transitioned to my home with the expectation of becoming eligible for adoption and I desperately hoped to become her adoptive mother. Yet, many months after she arrived her birth family's rights had still not been terminated. Her birthmother, incarcerated and unable to care for her daughter, was surrendering her rights. Her birthfather promised to appeal involuntary termination. Hopeful, but certain, I offered Rae the best reassurance I could. I promised to try and make her my forever daughter.

Together we dreamed of adoption day. That day came in October of 2003. My forever daughter is my "Rae" of sunshine and we have become a family in the best sense, even adding a little brother to our nest. On my birthday, Courtney Rae gave me a note:

Dear Mom,
I thank you for fixing my life so neatly. I thank you very sweetly. I'm glad I have a mom like you.
Love, Courtney

I replied:
Dear Courtney Rae,
I've never been happier in my whole life. I'm so glad I have you for my daughter. Thank you!
Love, Mom

—*Wilma Ice,* Virginia

Author's Note: While writing this story Courtney's name was 'Courtney Rae Johnson.' After the adoption finalization, she became 'Courtney Irene RosaLee Ice.' A fact both Courtney and her mother, Wilma, are very proud to report! —*MMB*

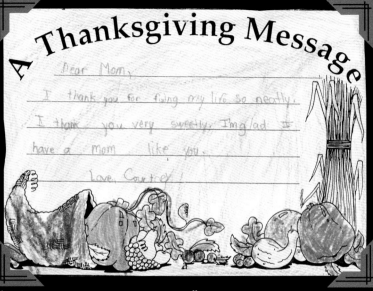

A Thanksgiving Message

Dear Mom,

I thank you for fixing my life so neatly.

I thank you very sweetly. I'm glad I

have a mom like you.

Love, Courtney!

"Dear Mom...Love, Courtney."

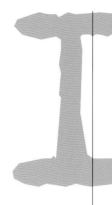

**"I know there is a child waiting for us to find him,"
I cried as I shared this testimony with others in my
church on a Sunday that I will never forget.**

Monday morning I awakened to a feeling of great urgency. I readied our five children for their day and began moving swiftly, almost strategically, through our home. Room by room, I cleaned and organized while my husband prepared himself for the workday ahead. I heard the phone ring and I knew it was the call that would change our lives. My husband came downstairs and told me Social Services was on the line and that a baby was waiting at the local hospital.

I was told the baby was sick with high drug and alcohol levels. As I listened, there was no reservation on my part and I offered to drive to the hospital immediately. We rushed to the nursery with camera and blanket in hand. There we saw the caseworker, a sweet and gentle lady, with teary eyes, holding a tiny baby. We walked over to her and, without words, she handed a little angel to me and I cried tears of joy.

**When moms, like me, can no longer bring babies
into the world, God finds ways to deliver them to us.**
A caseworker followed us home and we gave her a tour of the house. When she left, members of our church came to see the baby and to bless him. There was a powerful sense of peace in our home that day.

When our five children arrived home from school, each came quietly up to the baby. We decided to name him Aaron and from day one, our children helped care for his every need.

Aaron was born with one of the highest drug and alcohol levels of any baby ever born at our local hospital, yet with love and care, he has never experi-

enced a single drug withdrawal. He is healthy and strong and has defeated each and every bump in the road that he has encountered.

Aaron is a beautiful baby! His spirit shines so brightly. Aaron's adoption was finalized in February of 2004. Looking back, I can say the road has not always been easy, but I want to stress that nothing could be more rewarding.

Fostering and adopting children is about compassion and an unwavering commitment to make a difference.

As I move forward as a mother, I work to see that my children grow and learn a powerful lesson: that love and compassion start at home and make the world a better place.

On that Sunday in church, my cries were heard and the lives of everyone in my family have been blessed beyond words.

—*Rebecca and Luke Armstrong,* Colorado

Remember and Love

Courtney

My daughter hasn't seen her birthmother in nearly three years. Her fading memories seem to bring about anger and fear. She will ask, "How can I love my mommy if I can't remember important things about her?"

I have seen Courtney's birthparents several times in court. After each hearing, I tell my daughter that I've seen her parents and then I invite her to ask me any questions she might have. "What does my mommy look like?" I describe a tall, pretty woman with shoulder length hair and then she tearfully stops me and blurts out, "I already knew that!"

A few moments later, a hesitant and tearful little voice asks, "Does my mommy still wear a lot of make-up?" "What kind of shoes did she have on?" Stalling for time, I take a deep breath and say, "Today she wasn't wearing any make-up because your mommy is in jail." I continue, "Everyday she wears an orange shirt, orange pants, and shoes that are flat and soft." Courtney's lip quivers as she tries not to cry.

If I watch her closely, Courtney's actions ask the questions she hasn't yet found words for. Questions like, "How can I love all of my mommies?" Sorting through the confusion, her actions beg for explanation: "There is my real mommy who gave birth to me, my real foster mommy who I remember most, my other foster mommy who didn't keep me very long, Grandma, and now my almost adoptive mommy who wants to keep me forever."

Courtney seems to sense the inherent rejection of not being able to live with the mother whose tummy she grew in. Occasionally, she implies that she had to move because she didn't behave or perhaps forgot to do some assigned chore.

I took Courtney to visit her birthmother's old house where strangers live now. The house is now red but used to be white, as my soon-to-be adopted daughter points out. She sees her grandpa's old shed and the bare spot on the ground where the doghouse used to be. She also notices the stairs that her stepfather pushed her little sister down. Then my brave little girl sees the bushes in the backyard where she hid with her little sister one cold and scary night because her mommy was angry and forbade her to go inside the house.

Encouraging Courtney to make decisions on how she wants to remember her birth family seems of critical importance. I have a foster son who is two and my daughter will say, "Mommy, when Koty gets big he's going to think you're the only mommy he's ever had. He won't remember anybody else!" These thoughts seem to make Courtney happy and sad at the same time. I understand those feelings.

You see, remembering ALL of their families is how children adopted from foster care maintain their roots. I reassure my daughter that we can remember her other families in lots of ways. We send birthday cards to her birthparents along with Mother's Day and Father's Day cards. We mail pictures of Courtney, along with report cards, and always include her birth family in mealtime and bedtime prayers. Our address and phone number have been shared and invitations to visit have been extended although, each gesture has gone unanswered.

The time may come when Courtney will choose to remember in a different way. I will be ready to follow her lead when that moment arrives.

Whatever happens, my children and I have become a loving and remembering family. Our earliest concepts of family were formed in foster care. I grew up there. My mother grew up there. I have parented only children from the foster care system. I don't know much about traditional or nuclear families and neither do my children.

Family, foster or otherwise, is about belonging. Remembering helps our family create a sense of belonging.

I have learned that foster families must protect memories—often distinguishing the good from the bad and harvesting strength from deep wounds. It is when we build new and warm experiences as part of a remembered family that we heal, grow and expand our capacity to love.

My children ride on my back as I gallop around the yard. We laugh as I make funny noises and flip them upside down. Courtney, my beautiful adopted daughter, loves when I pretend she is a baby and say, "Are you my big, little girl?" We are creating our own happy memories to last a lifetime.

—Wilma Ice, Virginia
Author's Note: While writing this story Courtney's name was 'Courtney Rae Johnson.' After the adoption finalization, she became 'Courtney Irene RosaLee Ice.' A fact both Courtney and her mother, Wilma, are very proud to report! *—MMB*

Out of The Blue

Perhaps many people can say what I am about to say: when I first began fostering children I had no plans of adopting. I was experiencing a bit of the 'empty nest syndrome' and wanted little ones in my home once more. I also wanted to foster children on my own terms with the choice to stop when I felt that the time had come.

I received a phone call from a social worker asking if I wanted to foster a baby who was still in the hospital. I immediately said, "Yes." The social worker began informing me of the baby's health condition. "This baby was born three months premature, weighs only four pounds at six weeks of age, and has tested positive for crack and alcohol." She added, "The baby needs to be picked up today." I raced out of my house and headed to the hospital to meet a tiny little girl.

She was the cutest, most adorable baby I had ever seen. We were inseparable. I would hold her close, feeding her every three hours in order to give her the calories she needed to grow. However, I would remind myself that this situation might not last, as the baby's birthmother wanted all four of her children back. As a foster parent, I needed to ready myself for 'goodbye.'

After a year, though, it seemed apparent that this baby girl would be staying with us. We adopted our precious little angel when she was not yet two years of age.

I have raised three biological sons and now have adopted a girl. I could not love one more than the other and it does not matter that my daughter is not 'blood of my blood.'

She is my life, my heart and my soul. My daughter, almost five years old now, can cheer me up just by saying a couple of words. There is not a day that goes by when I don't look up at the sky and thank God for bringing this child to me, from out of the blue.

—*Debi Cantu,* Texas

On soft blue paper my foster mother, in England, documented how I loved to sit outside in my pram and how I didn't like my bath, adding she hoped my forever family would enjoy caring for me as she had. Then my foster mother wrote, "we all love her." These words are from a woman whose name and face I do not remember. Yet, these are words I will never forget from a woman I will always love.

—*Michelle Madrid-Branch,* New Mexico

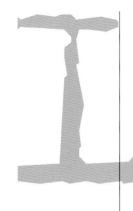

Leighann holds out her arms and enthusiastically says, "Daddy, Daddy, Daddy." When I am in that moment, I know that I made the right decision.

My wife had two children, ages 6 and 11, from a previous marriage and we wanted to add to our family by having a baby together. Only, my wife and I were unable to conceive and we began looking at other options. Adoption made the most sense to us and we contacted the Department of Children and Families.

We began the required steps which included background checks, inspections, personal interviews, and a ten-week training course known as M.A.P.P.*

In the course of one year, twenty-seven children came through our home, but only one stayed – Leighann. She was seven weeks premature at birth and was diagnosed with F.A.S.* (known as Fetal Alcohol Syndrome). Leighann weighed all of four pounds when she arrived at our house.

After roughly eight months with us, Leighann's biological parents had their parental rights terminated.* This development was our opportunity to adopt Leighann.

At this point, my marriage was suffering as my wife felt I was dedicating too much time to Leighann. An ultimatum was given and I chose to stand by my little girl. This child had already been let down by her biological parents and I was not going to do the same. My wife took her two children and walked away from our marriage. I was now a thirty-four year old single man with a one-year old baby girl.

Most of my friends said I was crazy to keep Leighann and even the Department of Children and Families tried to stop me. The department felt a single guy shouldn't raise a baby girl. I knew I had a fight on my hands, but I refused to give up, and with the help of my family I proved my capability of being a good father to Leighann.

I began the adoption process all over again through the Children's Home Society (CHS) and received tremendous support. The folks at CHS could clearly see how happy Leighann was with me and how we were a healthy family that belonged together.

Adoption Day arrived during the summer of 2003. It was one of the happiest days of my life. Leighann has gone through so much but those challenges are now a part of her past.

Everyday when I come home, Leighann runs to me with open arms yelling "Daddy, Daddy, Daddy." When she hugs me, I cannot help but think about the wise decision I made. I lost a marriage with that decision, but I gained much more.

I thank God everyday for bringing my little girl into my life. She is my daughter and I knew that from the first moment I held her in my arms and saw those bright blue eyes shining back at me.

I only wish all children in waiting could experience this type of happy ending. Leighann's life is full of laughter. She will never be alone.

—*Melvyn Duprey,* Florida

*See Termination of Parental Rights (TPR) and definitions of M.A.P.P. and F.A.S. in the Glossary of Terms.

Son of My Heart

George

George was said to be a child who had trouble connecting with people. I was working at an agency providing support to foster children when I was made aware of an eight-year old boy who needed a suitable home. George was a survivor of physical abuse at the hands of his dysfunctional family. He needed a home that could cope with the special needs of a youngster still dealing with his traumatic past. My agency conducted many interviews with potential foster homes as it diligently worked to find the 'right fit' for George.

The 'right fit' came when I realized that I could offer this child the kind of support he so desperately needed. I became licensed to be a foster parent specifically to take care of George.

When he walked into what was now 'our' home, George peered through the door of one of the bedrooms and said, "This must be my room because all my stuff is here." Later that evening as we sat on the couch watching TV, he leaned over and whispered, "I already feel like I'm your son." His heartfelt message brought tears to my eyes and a lump to my throat as I thought of the incredible journey the two of us were embarking on together.

The first few months of this journey came with many adjustments as I suddenly became the single mother of an 8-year old boy with lots of issues. If I raised my voice, he expected to be hit and experienced flashbacks to a life of abuse by his biological parents. I learned to keep an even tone to my voice during moments of discipline, and eventually George learned that being beaten does not follow verbal corrections.

George was expected to be in my home for eight months while his mother received treatment and education on how to handle her son's behavioral needs. Eight months passed and soon after, George and I found ourselves celebrating a one year anniversary by the ocean.

As we entered our second year together, I was asked if I would consider guardianship or possibly adoption, as George's biological mother was not making sufficient progress to regain custody of her son. "Whoa," I replied, and then added I would have to seriously consider this lifetime commitment. This commitment, I knew, would totally and forever change my life since another human being would depend on me until adulthood. I was crazy about George and my extended family was fond of him too. Still, my thoughts focused on a forever commitment that I wasn't sure I was ready to make.

As we celebrated our two-year anniversary together I knew my hesitation needed to come to an end. George was part of my life and part of my family and so I asked to be considered as a permanent home. I began the process of upgrading from a foster home to a foster/adopt home. George's biological parents had their parental rights terminated* shortly after our two year anniversary, and finally, he was free to be adopted.

Now, as we near our three-year anniversary as a family, the adoption process is in the final stages of completion. I cannot envision what my life would be like without George. He is the son of my heart. It has been a long road with many choices and changes along the way. I never expected to end up as "Mom" when we started our journey together, although George tells me he always knew he always belonged with me. Ah, the faith and clear vision of a child!

We are a family now and, while I don't expect the road ahead to be without obstacles, George and I have proven that we are versatile enough to meet the challenges. George has been embraced by my entire family for the valuable human being he is and I've never seen his smile as bright as it is today. He is a happy child.

George asked me if, after his adoption, he could change his middle name along with his last name. I said I thought that was possible and then asked, "What do you want to change your middle name to?" George replied, "I want to be named after my new grandpa, Charles." I smiled and thought, "it seems my father will have a namesake after all."

And this final note: George and Charles had four wonderful years together before my dad passed away. Upon my father's death, George commented to me, "We have each other." I know that without my son in my life the grief would be even greater. My father will always be missed. My son and I will move forward together, understanding the blessing of our time spent as a family. We will always remember the power of my dad's connection with his grandson. George will carry the spirit of his grandfather with him forever.

—*Lori N. Patterson,* Washington State

* See Termination of Parental Rights (TPR) found in the Glossary of Terms.

Michael's Gifts

Michael suffered his first heart attack quietly. We were in the middle of preparations for pre-adoptive placements of eleven-year old Missy and twelve-year old Brandon. One of Mike's biggest concerns was that these two children would not be allowed to come into our home and stay, if he was ill.

Family always meant the world to Mike and he absolutely abhorred the separation of siblings. You see, Mike grew up in 'kinship care,' and was raised by a loving, but stressed grandmother, and an alcoholic grandfather. Mike's twin brothers and his sister were placed for adoption and they didn't see each other again until all were in their forties. Unfortunately for them, it was too late to form solid relationships.

Four days after Missy and Brandon came into our home, Mike had his second heart attack — the one he would not survive. I phoned Social Services from the hospital and asked if the children could stay with me as a single parent, and they agreed.

There was an immediate change in my relationship with Missy and Brandon that day. An instant bond was formed and the hugs and kisses, along with the tears, flowed.

Missy and Brandon sat in the family room area of the hospital writing an obituary with me, for the father they had only known a short time. Within the obituary, they saw their names listed as our children. This had a profound impact on both of them as it became crystal clear that they were our children. That day everything changed as Michael's love was truly felt all around us. Missy and Brandon experienced a powerful sense of belonging to a family.

The law says that adopted children may take the last name of their adoptive parent. Even though I use my maiden name, Missy and Brandon are challenging the law to also take Michael's last name. His connection to them will be seen every time they sign a paper or write a letter. Acquiring his last name is a tribute to Mike's life that these children want to make happen. He will live within them forever.

And as for me, everyday I wake to the beautiful gifts Michael left behind: our beautiful children whom he wanted so badly.

—*Kary Ledbetter,* Idaho

Following our seven-year plan, my husband and I moved to northern Wisconsin. We had been living in a suburban neighborhood of Minneapolis and dreamed of "living in the woods." After many trips to the area we now call home, we found employment and purchased 240 acres of land to build on. Our jobs in northern Wisconsin began before the Minnesota house sold. We put a small camper on our new property, which for a three-month construction phase became our living space. Our Wisconsin home was completed in November of 1991.

That winter, we met and spoke with new friends who were foster parents. They encouraged us to become licensed foster parents. My husband and I felt we had room in our hearts and in our home, so we looked into foster parenting. We were licensed in the spring of 1992.

Our first foster son came to us in June of that same year. Many children followed through the years, most of them returning to their birth families.

In July of 1995, a child named Ty was placed in our home. Ty had difficulty with physical mobility and wasn't able to utter any words. We dedicated ourselves to helping Ty get better and took him to speech therapy and physical therapy. He was part of our family for three months and was then returned to his biological family. However, nine months later, Ty's social worker called and asked if we would take Ty and his baby brother, Damen, into our home. Of course, we said yes. Ty resumed the speech and physical therapy sessions we had assisted him with months before.

Little Damen was so afraid of many things and he screamed much of the time. He had a fear of water and darkness and anything furry. He did not want to be held. We worked with a therapist and began using brushing and holding techniques with both boys, which produced amazing results. Slowly, both boys began to trust us and allowed us to be close to them.

Ty and Damen were our foster boys for a period of five years and were returned to their biological family on two occasions during that time frame. Both boys attended an Early Education program at their school and both saw a therapist once a week. Ty received speech and physical therapy through school professionals. Ty was diagnosed with Asperger Syndrome*. No one could determine if Ty was unable to mentally form and say words, or if he just couldn't understand what was being said to him. As for Damen, his screaming episodes happened less and less.

Ty and Damen were fortunate to have a caring guardian looking out for their best interests. The county we live in had filed only one Termination of Parental Rights petition* in the boys' history. The attorney representing Ty and Damen, filed for termination in August of 2000, and after many hearings and eventually a trial, the parents' rights were officially terminated.

On one occasion, I took Ty to his therapy appointment and asked his therapist if she could think of a way to talk to Ty and have him respond. We wanted to know if he understood that we planned to adopt him and his brother. The therapist took Ty with her to her playroom. When they came back to the waiting room, the therapist said, "Ty is relieved." Knowing these couldn't be his words, I asked her what he said. "I don't have to worry anymore," were the words six-year old Ty had finally spoken. Damen, at five-years of age, spoke very well and told us that he was very happy we would adopt him and Ty.

My husband and I adopted both boys in May of 2001. Ty taught himself how to read that summer and when he began school the next fall, he was reading at the top of his class. We have always felt that permanence is most important for all children. Our sons' experiences reinforce that feeling.

P.S. We have also adopted a little girl named Maria. Ty and Damen adore their sister and she is their biggest fan. Friends and family often comment on how well our kids get along. My husband and I have two adult sons. Our younger children and our older sons are many years apart in age, but when we get together, we see one happy family. Damen summed up his feelings to us one evening on the way home from a church Christmas program. He said, "Thanks for taking us to the program. I love you, mom and dad. I am happy you adopted us. We didn't have parents and you didn't have children."

—*Anne Rankin,* Wisconsin
*Definitions of Asperger Syndrome and Termination of Parental Rights (TPR) can be found in the Glossary of Terms.

Chris Boffa's Ride

Bobbie and I shared a powerful dream. We met in 1971 and, to others, it seemed like we came from different planets. I was from Rhode Island and she was from Alabama. What attracted us to each other was a common passion for life and a common belief that, together, we could make a difference in the world. Our dream was to, someday, adopt a child.

In October of 1973, our daughter Cathy was born. She was a healthy baby but the toll the delivery took on Bobbie was, in a word, frightening. Six months later, we learned the reason for this difficulty in childbirth. Bobbie was diagnosed with an inverted uterus and we were told that another pregnancy could result in the death of baby, mother, or both. My wife underwent a hysterectomy and we sought the assistance of Catholic Family Services. We were ready to adopt!

The caseworker asked us many questions about the type of child we were interested in. What age? Would we be willing to accept a child with disabilities? We answered, "We'll adopt an older child, one with mild to moderate disabilities. In other words, we want a child who would not find love without us."

A book of photographs was placed in front of us with children of all ages, shapes, and colors. These were the special needs kids of Alabama, we were told, and then the caseworker asked, "What do you think?" Adding, "Take a few weeks and let us know if you still believe this is an option for you."

We called back the very next week, as our hearts were responding to a picture of a little boy, standing on a well-worn couch and waving to the camera with a big smile on his face. "Oh, that's Chris," said the caseworker, "He's two and has many problems to overcome." She went on to explain that Chris hadn't learned to feed himself yet, could only walk with assistance and hadn't begun to speak. "You can meet him if you want." She added, "He's been passed over many times and may be a long-term child." "No," we replied, "we can help him carry his burdens and he'll be just fine."

It was three weeks before we would meet Chris. Those weeks felt like years! Finally, our family of three met the young boy in the photo. Though Chris was two years old, he was wearing size 18 months clothing. His big shiny eyes and his nametag seemed to dwarf all of his other features. That day, with Chris in tow, we left the Department of Human Resources holding all of his possessions in a brown paper bag. In that paper bag, was one diaper, a few photos and a list of all the things the State of Alabama said Chris would never accomplish.

Included on that list was that our son would never run or skip, speak any other words than a few garbled phrases, was borderline educationally and mentally retarded, and would likely be institutionalized someday.

Yet, Chris' smile was absolutely infectious. We brought him a stuffed bunny with his name sewn on it and he immediately hugged it. He then compared his nametag with that of his bunny's! Mother Angelica, foundress of EWTN TV, and her nuns asked what they could pray for and we said, "Pray that one day Chris will be able to say his own prayers and that one day he will be more like us."

For months, Chris had to be tied with dress ties to sit and eat and maintain his balance. His tiny legs were unable to keep him up for long. Little did we know how soon this would change!

Our daughter, Cathy, and her little brother, Chris, were inseparable. Cathy was always there to defend her brother and truly learned about love through Chris. Until he was six, Chris was taught to use a form of sign language to communicate and would, sometimes, throw temper tantrums due to frustration over his lack of speech. For many years, he would visit a speech pathologist as he slowly learned.

At fourteen, Chris was achieving many things. He was in Special Ed and learned to be a teacher's helper. One of Chris' main goals was to learn to drive his father's car. Every morning at 4:30,

photos courtesy Harvey Webb,
North Jefferson News

we would get up, hit the streets and commence driving lessons. After six months behind the wheel, Chris drove around a grocery store parking lot. After one year, he graduated to the high school parking area. Each and every Sunday he would say, "Okay dad—I drive. I did good."

When Chris turned seventeen, he took Driver's Ed and then was awarded his driver's license. He also received a part-time job as a sacker at the very grocery store we drove around for years.

The year 2004 marked a major milestone in Chris' life. He has never learned to tell time, read or comprehend the value of money. But he has learned to save! Chris has saved most of his paychecks, tips, and birthday money. He saved enough to not only buy the car he now drives to work, but in February 2004 Chris purchased his own home!

Have we made a difference in Chris' life? We believe so. And I know Chris has made a difference in ours.

Funny, after all these years, we can still see Chris driving down the road with his big red car tag that reads: BOFFA'S RIDE!

—*Bob Boffa,* Alabama

"He (Chris) saved enough to not only
buy the car he now drives to work, but
in February 2004 Chris purchased his
own home!"

Voices From Foster Care

I Am Jelani

He was an eight-year old boy walking home alone at two o'clock in the morning. That was a 'routine' happening for this child whose mother was afflicted by mental illness and whose father existed only as a name on a birth certificate. There was no mommy and daddy tucking this little boy into bed at night; no parents kissing him gently on the head and then turning out the lights.

Jelani's young world was filled with challenges no one should have to face. His mother was eventually diagnosed with schizophrenia and hospitalized. With virtually no supervision, he followed a road of hopelessness filled with crime, a disregard for education, and the real possibility of either prison or death.

Circumstances put Jelani into the foster care system, but he was released back to his mother's custody after she was discharged from the hospital. Although she tried to take care of him, her mental illness controlled their lives. Jelani remembers only Thanksgiving at a homeless kitchen and living at a shelter for abused and battered women. After a few months, his mother was back in the hospital and Jelani was back in foster care.

Jelani was nine years old when he was placed with foster parents for whom he would grow a deep affection. In this home, he also had a foster brother, foster sisters, a roof over his head, his own room and enough food to eat. His foster family also came with aunts, uncles, and cousins who saw him as an important member of the family.

Life at home for Jelani was better than it had ever been, yet he was still caught up in old habits and continued to face problems at school. On the last day of 6th grade, he rushed to his home of two years only to find that his bags were packed. Jelani was being sent to a group home due to his behavioral problems in the classroom. His foster mother consoled him as he cried, explaining that the better he behaved in the group home the sooner he could return to them.

It was the summer of 1992 when Jelani entered the group home. There he found kids with far more serious problems than his own. He remembered the words of his foster mother and vowed to focus on getting back to her as soon as possible. At the end of that summer, Jelani was returned to his foster home. He never felt a true sense of security again. Part of his new routine was checking to see if his bags had been packed.

Within months of returning to his foster home, he was informed that he was returning to his biological mother who had regained her parental rights. So, at the age of 12, he followed his sense of duty and responsibility and went with her. Within a couple of weeks, Jelani knew it was not a beneficial situation for either of them, so he called his social worker and asked to be returned to his foster family.

Jelani's decision crushed his mother and it also left him with unresolved feelings of guilt. Struggling with his emotions, he began having trouble again in school and was eventually sent to another group home. For the next year and a half, Jelani would survive in a boy's home that could easily be viewed as the preliminary step to adult prison. Fortunately, that experience changed his life forever and Jelani decided to take charge of his life forever. His improved behavior was duly noted and he was placed back with his foster family at the beginning of high school. Through these years, Jelani played football, made honor roll, and focused on going to college.

Life seemed to be moving along smoothly until Jelani's sixteenth year when he lost both of his foster parents. Their deaths, once again, forever changed his life. Over the next two years, he was bounced from the houses of relatives and friends. Jelani dug deep and found the strength to graduate from high school. He then went off to college and a life on his own which he would discover, had its own set of challenges.

The experiences of finding an apartment, a job, filing taxes and handling other financial matters, were large hurdles for Jelani to overcome. Unlike many of his college peers, he had no mom and dad to turn to for support. When his friends were heading home for Thanksgiving or Christmas break, Jelani was left alone with no forever family to visit. He worked three jobs to pay his way through school and after four years became a college graduate. It was a long arduous road.

The little boy who was once eight-years old and walking home alone at two in the morning was now sitting in a crowded auditorium waiting to receive his college diploma. As he sat there, he was communicating with the only family he truly knew: himself.

I am Jelani Freeman. As I sit with my college graduating class I have time to reflect on my life. I am heading to graduate school and know that my accomplishments to date are more than I ever imagined. I am Jelani Freeman and I aged out of foster care. I have persevered and cleared many hurdles on my way to this moment. As I look out at the audience, I know that no one has come to share in this amazing achievement with me. It is now that I truly realize how important a forever family is. Success without people around you who love and care for you is a lonely feeling.

Adoption never happened for Jelani but he wants it to happen for the thousands of children like him, who wait in foster care for their permanent homes. These children possess such potential and long for the forever love that is vital to us all. Jelani is doing his part in life to see that these kids aren't alone at their college graduation.

—*Jelani Freeman,* Washington, D.C.

Author's Note: I met Jelani Freeman in Washington, D.C. during the summer of 2003 while he was working in the office of Senator Hillary Rodham Clinton. Staff with the Congressional Coalition On Adoption Institute raved about this young man and his courage and strength. After getting to know Jelani, my heart simply melted for this human being who possesses such capacity to give back to those who are living in foster care today. His story of triumph over turmoil is and should be inspirational to us all. Today, Jelani works in the office of Mayor Anthony A. Williams of the District of Columbia. He serves as the Youth Engaged in Service (YES) Ambassador through a partnership with the Points of Light Foundation. Jelani is the coordinator of National Youth Service Day, supports the staff of the DC Youth Advisory Council and works with Learn and Serve programs. He is a living testimony of the beautiful potential that children in foster care carry with them. Jelani is a messenger for their needs.

—*MMB*

Additional comments from Jelani:
I want to thank Michelle Madrid-Branch for giving me the opportunity to be involved in this wonderful project and for her friendship, which I deeply value. I also would like to thank Jackie Booker who is my mentor and fairy godmother. My thanks to actress Victoria Rowell for her sisterly guidance and support. Last, but certainly not least, I thank Senator Hillary Rodham Clinton for the incredible opportunity to work with her and for helping me gain confidence within. Her on-going kindness and compassion leads me each day to a deeper understanding of my endless abilities.

—*JF*

"I am Jelani Freeman and I am committed to shedding light on the importance of adoption."

"To Jelani Freeman with appreciation."
-Hillary Rodham Clinton

Imagine being scared everyday of your life as you wonder which one of the kids would get a beating. Would it be me this time? Would I have to hide in a room while dad beats up mom, as I worry whether she would live through this one? Did I clean the house well enough? Was dinner good? Are the kids behaving or would I have to take a beating for one of them? Will mom and/or dad even make it home from the bar tonight?

I lived my life like this from as far back as I can remember, until one day, at the age of eleven, I decided I could not bear it any longer. On that day, I remember that my dad beat my mother so badly, I thought for sure she would die. I packed up some belongings in a trash bag, gathered my siblings and asked my mother if she was coming with us or staying.

Taking this brave stand, I embarked on a whole new life path. I spent the next year bouncing from hotel to hotel, while our mother worked and spent most of her time in a bar. Then mom disappeared for over a week with her boyfriend, and I found myself taking care of my siblings, as well as a twelve-year-old could. Someone finally called social services and I spent the next three years bouncing around to 14 different homes and shelters, within the foster care system.

When I was fifteen and pregnant, I finally found that special foster family who set my life on another path. I knew that I wanted a better life for my son and myself. I also knew that, at fifteen, I wanted to be a foster parent. I wanted to provide a better path for children in the foster care system than the one I had experienced. I wanted to let them know that they, too, could find that special family. At the age of twenty-one, I became the youngest foster parent in the state of Colorado.

My husband and I have three wonderful children: Jon is now eighteen years old. He's in the Army National Guard and is also working on getting his real estate license just like Mom! Lauryn is almost eleven and is the most loving and independent child you will ever meet. Austin is my nephew, whom we adopted into our family this year. He is a bundle of energy at the age of five. We also have three wonderful teenage foster daughters who keep us on the go! Providing foster care enables me to stay home with my children.

Over the past 14 years, Mike and I have provided care for over 212 foster children. We have been a receiving home, a group home, and now a family foster home. There are many wonderful stories to share. Being a foster parent, just as parenting our own, is a roller coaster ride of emotions I would not trade for anything in the world! For the past eight years, we have provided care for teenage girls, ages 13 to 18. People think I am crazy for taking on the older kids; however, that is where my passion is. It is what I am called to do. I tried to retire from foster parenting once, but it only lasted three months. Before I knew it, I had four girls and I am happy to be back on that roller coaster again.

There are so many children who need us, and so many children who need and want a family to provide love, stability and understanding. Former foster children, who are now young women, will come back to our home with great pride to share their families, their successes and their dreams with us. To know that we had a part in guiding, teaching and loving them, is the greatest reward in life. When they come back to say, "thank you for everything you have done," well, that is what life is all about.

Where would I be today if it weren't for my foster family? It was they who went to court on behalf of a fifteen-year-old mother and said that they would take care of me, and my new baby. They fought to keep us together. It was my foster family who taught me how to be a parent, how to love and be loved, and most importantly how to love myself.

If I can help one child overcome his fears, and feel loved like he has never felt loved before, then I have accomplished my mission. Imagine!

—*Tina Kulp,* Colorado

My Dear Foster Dad

Although I was not born your daughter, you made me your daughter when you invited me into your home and into your heart. I know I wasn't the easiest teenager. Did you know that you became my hero? Did you know that it was my dream to find a husband that would care for and love me and my child, as much as you loved us? You helped me break a painful cycle that I inherited from my biological family. Thank you. My life would not be what it is today, if it had not been for you.

You are a great role model of what a father should be and you have made the most important difference in my life and the lives of all the other children you have touched.

I love you.

—*Tina Kulp,* Colorado

The Ones that Matter, The Times that Count

Chris

My life has been a seemingly endless road of change. Some of the changes were small and others were large. Some were for the better and others were for the worse. Through all the ups and downs though, there have always been two constants in my life: my mother, Amy, and my father, Mike.

I first met Mike and Amy in November of 1992. I was in the sixth grade at Sunnyslope Elementary School, where Amy was a social worker. At that time, I was living with my Aunt Cynthia where I had been for almost six months. Shortly after celebrating my twelfth birthday, my Aunt decided she could no longer support me. She turned me over to Camelback Hospital for evaluation where I was examined and it was determined that my health, both physically and mentally, was too good to stay there.

I was transferred from Camelback Hospital to a shelter in the lowest income area of Phoenix, Arizona. I lived there with a handful of other unfortunate children who were just surviving in the same horrible conditions.

Sandy, my social worker and a colleague of Amy's, told her of my situation. Amy wanted to do something to help me and decided to spend some 'one on one' time with me. During my free time in school, I would go to her office and she would have food or candy waiting for me. Amy also arranged for me to spend time with her husband, Mike, and her father, Larry. The guys took me to a Phoenix Cardinals football game and Larry tried his best to spoil me. It was the greatest day of my life!

At that point, I had no idea what Amy and Mike were pondering. I would soon learn that my life was headed for a huge change, for the better. I remember my social worker, Sandy, pulling me out of class one day and leading me to her office.

"I have something to ask you," she said. I listened as she continued. "I told Amy and Mike about the shelter you are living in and they want you to come live with them. Do you want to do that?" My response took less than half a second, "Yes!" I responded with excitement.

Sandy, who always looked out for me, added, "Amy is going to pick you up after school today and take you to the shelter to get your belongings. Then you'll go live with her for awhile."

I could barely contain myself as I walked out of the shelter that afternoon. I will always remember the huge smile on my face. Even though my time in the shelter had lasted only three weeks, it seemed an eternity. Those were the worst three weeks of my life.

It was arranged that I would stay with Amy and Mike for a couple of weeks while we waited for a foster home to open up. The wait time turned into a year and then into two. The second year, Amy and Mike decided to become licensed foster parents so that I would have a place to call "home." I am certain I have caused many challenges and difficulties for my parents throughout the years, but they have always handled each challenge with dignity and love.

One memory will always be a pivotal one. I skipped school one day, in order to travel to Tucson and visit the Marine Corps Recruiting Station. I decided to join the Marines. Upon my return home, it was time to tell my parents of my plans. My mother was surprisingly happy as she felt a little discipline would be beneficial. My father, however, was hesitant. I could tell this was not the path he expected me to take, but he never told me it was the wrong decision. The last thing I wanted was to let him down.

When I graduated from Boot Camp, my family was there to greet me. I was ecstatic to have accomplished such a feat. My father, Mike, came up to me and shook my hand saying, "Congratulations, you did it."

I have been the child of Amy and Mike's for nine years and they have helped me out more than I ever knew parents could. It is my intention to live my life in a way that demonstrates to them how well they did.

—*Chris Vinzant,* United States Marine Corps, Iraq

Author's Note: Chris is part of the Bulk Fuel unit in Iraq. His foster parents, Mike and Amy SanRoman, say they just smile when they think of the boy, back in 1992, whom seemingly no one in America wanted, is now so proud to defend his country. I salute Chris Vinzant and ask us all to remember the thousands of amazing young people in foster care today. A forever home can turn their lives around. —*MMB*

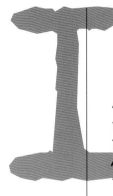

I'll be Home for Christmas

"I'll be home for Christmas,
You can count on me.
They'll be snow and mistletoe
And presents under the tree"
—Walter Kent, Kim Gannon, Buck Ram (1946)

She stood at the window looking at the falling flakes. Thinking. Alone. Our house was a bustle, the tree was decorated, holiday music filled the air. We had already baked a batch of ginger cookies. The sounds, sights and smells expressed Holiday spirit and festivity. The children expressed varying degrees of anxiety over the coming holiday.

Some were emotionally dead from past life experiences and looked toward the holidays with mistrust and suspicion. Others ran from surprise to new experience exclaiming shrieks of joy, mixed with apprehension. Were the presents under the tree 'really' theirs to keep? Were the BIG presents only for MY children? Were they ONLY going to get clothes? My heart ached for each of them to feel that the shining star at the top of the tree was reachable in each of their lives. Each child was special and each had a reason for being. This was the season of the year that I felt joy and completeness.

The girl at the window turned. Her eyes silently said: I don't care how much you know about my family and me. I need to know how much you care 'about' and 'for' me. I can't tell you my past holidays. It is hell to tell. I want to be a part of your celebration and joy, but I am scared. I don't know how to be and I miss my family.

My heart cried for this young woman. Change and transition were excruciating to her. Her old holiday experiences were familiar. In the chaos of her life she had knit a holiday family story that let her mind wander – the color of the wrapping paper, the ham her mom had baked, the bits and pieces of beauty and warmth and love – the hug from her cousin. And

I realized she had sealed away the pain and hurt and disappointment she had felt each year. I wanted to scoop her in my arms and tell her things don't always turn out like we planned, but that doesn't mean it turns out wrong. At that moment I knew that a hug or touch from me would feel invasive of her private thoughts – a collision of her memories, dreams and wishes with the reality of holidays in my home. I headed for the kitchen and returned with hot chocolate garnished with red and green mini marshmallows. "I brought you some hot chocolate," was all I said and together we silently sipped and watched the flakes fall. The gift of the moment; togetherness wrapped in the peace and respect of silence. And the young woman wished upon the falling flakes, Oh let me be home for Christmas.

For over twenty Christmases and three hundred children I had finally learned to shut up at least for a while. My resilient new foster daughter sipped her cocoa. I thought of the child I had just brought home for the holidays whose eyes pleaded with me to stay.

In another home her birthmother looked out the window at the falling flakes. She wondered where her daughter was. Was she happy? Was she lonely? Her heart ached. The pain of having her children absent during the holidays never departed. Every Sunday at church she looked at the empty seats and asked God why life had to go this way? And she hoped in the deepest part of her heart that someone with compassion held her daughter and cared for her. And she prayed that her daughter wouldn't forget her no matter what had happened and that she knew how much she was loved. Yes she could keep her daughter in her heart, but that wasn't the same as a hug. And she also knit together a holiday family story that danced in her mind. Happy memories of Christmas past; Oh, if only her daughter could be home for Christmas.

A child zoomed past like a freight train, chasing another youngster. His behavior had gone into warp speed at the sound of the first Christmas Carol. Every word I spoke returned to me twisted and tormented. There was nothing I could do right. There was nothing in my home that would feel like the holidays. He had assured me, "I will be home by Christmas!"

At another window, a mother stood despondent, holding her beer and joint – those damn flakes only make life worse. What kind of Christmas is this? My kids are gone. The system stole them from me. Her chemical dependency had come at such a cost. The system let me down, they weren't there when I needed them. Her heart ached and her anger raged – at the system and my home. It was too painful to see the reflection of her actions and life and its gift to the present circumstances she faced. She wanted her kids back and she wanted them back now. The holidays held little meaning without her kids. And she fantasized about the food and tree and presents, when in reality they did not exist beyond her mind. She hurt. Her mind scattered through thoughts of holiday cheer and holiday horror. She would find a way to be with her children. They will be home for Christmas, she thought, as she formulated a plan of return.

Holidays are a time of pain and confusion for the families of children in out-of-home care. As caregivers we must proceed through the holidays with caution and love. We must respect and remember the families of origin of children in our care. We must remember there is another "Home For Christmas." Some families share a special meal together. Some bake cookies. Some get approved special visitations for children to see their families. Don't forget to share the holiday gifts they may make in school. Take some time to write cards or make ornaments. Take time to shop for presents or make gifts for siblings and family of origin. Consider making a dish to give when the children visit (and include the plate in the gift). Make a small package of holiday cheer – bath soaps, shampoos, candles, hot pad holders. Wrap everyday items that can be used and enjoyed. Reach out. Don't leave that birth family isolated. Let them know you care. Keep yourself safe and take care of the children. Let there be *two homes* for *Christmas!*

Bless You.

—Judy Howell, President MFCA
Reprinted with permission from *Our Families*
Author's Note: Judy Howell is the President of Minnesota Foster Care Association. She is an adoptive, foster and birthmother.

How a Kid Should Feel

Kelley

It wasn't the kind of farm you'd see if you drove I-90 across the South Dakota prairie: corn rolling in neat rows and a grain silo, a red barn, and a little white farmhouse situated close together for refuge from the prairie winds. Not at all; in fact, this was a muddy pig farm tucked away down a two-lane dirt road a few miles from where the legends of the Wild, Wild West—Wild Bill Hickok, Calamity Jane, and Jesse James came from, along with the beauty of the Black Hills that kept the local economy barely alive. The sky was big, the sun shone most days of the year, and the air was filled with the sweetness of clover. The year was 1976.

The farm's owners were short, happy people who had been raised in South Dakota; they were farmers just as their parents had been. They were also foster parents for a year to my brother and me when I was five and he was four. What I remember most about that place is the food and the animals— often the same thing—the "skin" on top of the milk straight from the cow, the bacon from a pig slaughtered the previous day, and a chicken from the coop for Thanksgiving dinner. All of which I refused to eat. The farm was a perfect place for mischief: eating cow food on a dare, playing "pigs" in the mud, and sneaking to a nearby field to find clay targets the adults missed when they shot skeet.

I wasn't sure who my mother was or what she looked like, but I had a magical inkling that she just might be Angie Dickinson, a.k.a. Police Woman; I couldn't be sure. I didn't know much about my father either: he had been living in Montana since I was two. What I did know for certain, though, was that I wanted more than anything to be with my sisters; my brother and I had known them as our caretakers, and we had been living in foster care without them for more than two years. My brother and I spent a weekend with them once while we were living on the farm. I pretended all weekend that we were a family, and that their foster parents were mine. When the weekend ended, I decided I wouldn't return to the farm without a fight. I grabbed my brother, ran with him to the foster parents' station wagon, jumped in, and locked all the doors. The keys were in the ignition. My sisters, their foster parents, and our social worker gathered around the car.

"Open the door!" they demanded.

I crossed my arms and fixed my eyes on the seat in front of me.

"Unlock the door!"

"No!"

"We'll give you a candy bar if you come out."

Hmm...tempting...but "No!"

Realizing I wouldn't budge, they tried my brother. When I saw him pull the lock, I yanked him toward me. He elbowed me and scrambled into the front seat. "Help me, help me," he giggled, as he unlocked the door and jumped out of the car. The social worker, tall and thin with black and white hair, pulled me out. "I'm sorry, you have to go back," he whispered. One sister rode back with us, and I sat on her lap and sobbed, my face buried in her shoulder.

A few weeks later everything changed. Our foster parents told us, "The people your sisters are living with would like you to come live with them. We want you both to know that we'd like to keep you and have you as our own children if you'd like that." We left the farm on a hot August night, the short-sleeves-and-shorts-all-the-way-up-until-bedtime kind of night. It was Friday, and all I knew was that sometime Friday afternoon we were leaving. Our clothes and toys were packed in black plastic bags stacked in the truck bed. I watched the clock. Finally at 8:30 pm I demanded to know when we were leaving. My foster mother told me to sit at the kitchen table and gave me a doughnut; 8:45 pm, another doughnut. She turned away to the sink, and I could tell from her shoulders she was crying.

But my dream had come true. We arrived at our new foster home, a small house on a small hill, and were greeted by a brown dachshund, our new foster parents, and our three sisters. It was almost dark, and I was feeling shy. I could barely talk. Kids were lingering in the driveway next door, watching us, motioning to us.

"We're cousins, y'know," the neighbor boy said.

"We are?"

"Remember, you used to live with our aunt and uncle."

"That was our old foster home."

"So you're going to live here now?"

"Uh huh. We get to live with our sisters."

We were tired. It was late, and our new mother led us to our new twin beds. Our first days there she held us, sang lullabies, and made blueberry muffins; she was 22 years old and worked as a Head Start teacher. Our new father was 23 years old and worked as a homebuilder. To me they were perfect.

Weeks passed, and our sisters became our sisters again as their roles as caretakers disappeared. The months turned into a year, and we all moved to a neighboring town. We settled in and became a family; not the perfect family I'd dreamt of, but a family that I knew as mine. I remember the day that I knew this: I was walking the few blocks home from school, shivering from the cold because the snow had soaked through my boots and the plastic bread bags meant to keep my feet dry. I trudged across the neighbor's lawn through knee-high snow. The sky was so dark from the approaching storm that my house, with its light shining through the frosted windows, had a soft yellow glow. When I entered the warm house, my foster mother smiled, hugged me, and handed me a mug of homemade hot chocolate. I joined my siblings in the kitchen feeling like I'd always imagined a kid should feel.

—*Kelley Cook Donovan,* Texas

"I've brought you a new playfellow," the fairy said. "You must be very kind to him and teach him all that he needs to know in Rabbitland, for he is going to live with you..."

And she kissed the little Rabbit again and put him down on the grass.

"Run and play, little Rabbit!" she said.

The endearing classic tale of *The Velveteen Rabbit: How Toys Become Real,* by Margery Williams, tells the tale of a beloved plush rabbit that belongs to a young boy and a beloved old rocking horse that teaches the little rabbit about "What Real Really Means."

Our family is a real family, though we do not share genetics or bloodlines. Children in our family have come from far and wide and, to each of the children who come under my care, I try hard to fulfill the role of a real mom.

I love the laughter of a child. I love the funny things they say and do. I cherish the quiet moments as they sleep. I grieve with them as they cry tears of loneliness, hurt and loss. My own tears flow along with theirs. I love watching them grow, learn and challenge the world from which they have come, as they become real. I try to encourage them to know themselves better, to give them permission to become their real selves, so that they eventually have the ability to function as healthy adults and, hopefully, as parents someday.

"What is real?" asked the Rabbit one day...

"Real isn't how you are made," said the Skin Horse. "It's a thing that happens to you. When a child loves you for a long, long time, not just to play with, but REALLY loves you, then you become Real."

Being part of a real family means that, no matter what happens in life, you do what is necessary to take care of each other. You stop doing what you want to do and do what you need to do, in order to keep your family safe. Often, it takes hard work and at times it even hurts. As the leaders of the family, you instill into each younger family member, the abilities to ensure a better future for that special person.

"Does it hurt?" asks the Rabbit.

"Sometimes," said the Skin Horse, for he was always truthful. "When you are Real you don't mind being hurt."

A real family is willing to change bad habits in order to remain healthy. A real family understands that change is a beautiful part of life and that nothing can ever remain the same. A real family embraces a new member and applauds the success of a member leaving for an independent future. A real family is there in the good times and in the bad times.

Real moms and dads love their kids and put a high priority on the needs of their children. A real mom or dad is willing to give up things so that those they care for can have a happy life. It has nothing to do with genetics but it has everything to do with time, love, care and compassion. A real mom or dad is not afraid of discipline. They understand the difference between needs and wants and are willing to take a hard stand if necessary.

"Does it happen all at once, like being wound up," he asked "or bit by bit?"

"It doesn't happen all at once," said the Skin Horse. "You become. It takes a long time. That's why it doesn't often happen to people who break easily, or have sharp edges, or who have to be kept carefully. By the time you are Real, most of your hair has been loved off, and your eyes drop out and you get loose in the joint and very shabby. But these things don't matter at all, because once you are Real you can't be ugly, except to the people who don't understand."

Over 300 different children have passed through the doors of my home, slept in my bedrooms and eaten at my table. There was nothing unreal about these children. Each came to my home under different circumstances. Thus, I expected nothing less of myself than to be a real mother and provide a real family for the children under my care.

In this time of rethinking large institutional care of children, I am saddened and apprehensive. Every child needs to have one human being, preferably two, who thinks that this child is the most special, fabulous, amazing, and wonderful person on earth. Birth parents do that. Relatives do that. Adoptive parents do that and many foster parents do that. Children can tell the difference between 'family-like' and family.

Can a career caregiver who receives a paycheck provide the love and care our foster and adoptive homes do? Foster care covers expenses, and adoption subsidy barely offsets the expenses of care. Can an orphanage provide a place to 'come home to' for holidays or crisis? The Minnesota institutional employee turnover is high. When a career caregiver goes on to a new career and leaves institutional care, does that mean the family is no longer? Or is this 'family-like' way of working with children acceptable? Real children thrive on long-term relationships and commitment.

Today I am a real grandmother – to real birth grandchildren and real foster grandchildren, a real birthmother to two real children, a real foster mother to over 300 children, and a real adoptive mother to four teens. These real children return home, write and call; sometimes they stop in for a visit. Many are grown.

Each of my real children has a different life story of which I was allowed to play a part, hopefully letting each of them become a little more real because of my contribution to their lives.

Tell your friends and family we need more adoptive and foster homes for real children.

God Bless.

— *Judy Howell,* President MFCA, Minnesota
Author's Note: Judy Howell is the President of Minnesota Foster Care Association. She is an adoptive, foster and birthmother.

As children, we are often taught the importance of saying 'thank you' when someone is friendly, kind, generous, or thoughtful. It was the very act of extending a note of thanks that changed my life and the lives of many others.

My childhood was full of hardships. At six months old, I was placed in foster care for the first time, because my mother had abandoned me for two weeks. I would eventually be returned to her care, but this was only the beginning. I spent the next eleven years bouncing around between an unstable and abusive home, along with a string of foster homes. At the age of eleven, I was permanently placed in foster care when my mother went to jail for drug and sexual abuse charges. I spent the next five years in a downward cycle, moving from one foster home to another, experiencing severe behavioral problems, and struggling academically.

From the start of my education, I faced many problems. I repeated the second grade because I hadn't attended enough school and as a result hadn't learned to read and write. That was no way to begin an education, but unfortunately, it was the direction my education continued to follow. Fortunately, after many foster homes and various schools, the course of my education was altered. At the start of my freshmen year in high school, I found myself in another new home and school. At this point, I reflected back on the course of my life and the lives of others in my biological family, and saw myself walking in their footprints. I had an epiphany, if you will: At this moment, I knew I was going to do something more with my life. I realized the pain I had caused myself and the many others who had tried to help me along the way and I hated myself for it. I was done allowing my past to control me; no longer would I hide behind the veil of a dark past. I made the decision to be the first college educated professional in my family.

From that day on, I have worked tirelessly to improve my education and my future. At the start of my journey, I was well behind the educational level of my peers. In ninth-grade, it was estimated that I had the writing and reading skills of a sixth-grader, but I would not be discouraged. To meet my goal, I worked day-in and day-out with tutors, teachers and my foster mother to complete assignments and gain ground on the fundamental gaps in my knowledge. As amazing as it sounds, by the end of the first semester, I was achieving nearly perfect A's. In four years of high school, I transformed myself from a sixth-grade intellectual, to an Honor Student, a member of the National Honor Society, a 911 Peer Tutor, a student in the Upward Bound Regional Math/Science Program, a varsity athlete, and SADD/SMILE member. I was also working part-time as a bank teller and started a small home cleaning business to save money for college.

I could see my dream of becoming a college graduate on the horizon the day I was accepted into Champlain College; but the money I had been able to save was hardly enough to cover the cost of one semester. So I began the process of applying for scholarships. I was fortunate to receive over eight scholarships my first year. I was very touched that the scholarship foundations and some individuals had made such generous contributions to my future. So I wrote each and every scholarship foundation and individual contributor a thank-you letter. I wanted to tell them about my journey. I wanted to let them know how grateful I was and how much their gifts meant to a foster child.

And here is where I believe my story comes full circle. Little did I know that one of my thank-you letters would lead to the creation of a scholarship fund with over 1.5 million dollars! My thank you to Terry F. Allen, an entrepreneur from Ferrisburgh, Vermont touched his life and heart in a way that neither of us will forget. Soon, an exchange of letters and cards began, many of which would contain additional small gifts from Terry. Our letters made a difference, because they gave a successful businessman the chance to see where his gifts had gone and the dreams he had supported. One afternoon, as I sat studying for college finals, I received a phone call from the Marketing Director of Champlain College. She informed me that Terry had made a contribution to another scholarship fund and the college thought it would be a wonderful idea if I spoke at the unveiling, again thanking him.

The afternoon of the unveiling was a sunny one. I listened as the details of the scholarship fund were described and gasped when the announcer said, "The scholarship was established by an initial donation of one million dollars, by Terry F. Allen." I had no idea the donation was so large. The announcer continued, "Terry has decided to make this donation because of a thank-you letter he received from a Champlain College student who sits among us now, Sonja L. Kemp." My mind went blank and my eyes were hazy, as tears rolled down my cheeks. To this day, I can hardly remember making my way to the podium to speak, nor can I remember just what I said. After that day, I was consumed in learning more about the generosity of the human spirit from a flurry of newspaper articles, TV and radio interviews, and Champlain's commencement.

Terry had been given the honor of delivering the commencement speech the day I received my Associate's Degree in accounting. I listened to Terry announce that he would be increasing his donation to 1.5 million dollars, and that thirty students, for the next ten years, would benefit from my thank-you letter and his kindness!

I went on to achieve my Bachelor's Degree in Accounting and was offered a career as an Auditor at one of the top four public accounting firms in the world. During my four years in college, Terry contributed over 25% to the cost of my education! Without his generous support (and support from many others) I would not have been able to afford college. I owe my success to hard work, my foster family, Terry F. Allen, and a thank-you letter.

In the end, I learned three very important lessons: 1) My background and circumstances may have influenced who I am, but when all is said and done, I am responsible for who I become. 2) Never be afraid to ask for a helping hand, for no one can make the journey alone. 3) Always say thank-you. My simple thank-you letter changed my life and the lives of others, as well.

—*Sonja Kemp,* Vermont

Moving to MUST

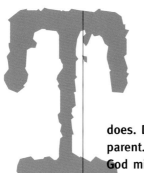

A Lesson from Dave

"The world works on families, it really does. Don't let fear stop you from being an adoptive parent. When you do the thing you fear the most, God might well have a pleasant surprise for you."
—*Dave's Way,* The Berkley Publishing Group, 1991, (p. 206) Dave Thomas (Founder of Wendy's International).

Dave Thomas is, quite frankly, my hero. If he were still alive, he'd likely shy away from the title I have assigned him. Truth is, he will always be of legendary stature to me. I was in my early twenties when I discovered that Mr. Thomas was, like me, a person of adoption. This realization was of profound importance because I saw a man who was successful and compelled to speak out with honesty and sincerity on the topic of being adopted. The year was 1990 and it seemed to me at a young age that adoption was finally out in the open.

Let's take a step back in time to the year 1932. This is the year when a young woman named Mollie, from Camden, New Jersey, would leave her hometown and head to Atlantic City. In a hospital there, Mollie gave birth to a child out of wedlock. She prepared an adoption plan. The baby, Dave Thomas, was adopted by a couple in Michigan.

The story, however, does not end there. Dave's adoptive mother died when he was five-years old. His adoptive grandmother, Minnie Sinclair, looked after Dave during the summer months and was responsible for shaping his beliefs on life. It was an outlook based on working hard, not cutting corners, enjoying your work, being true to your values, tackling challenges head-on, and praying. Dave's adoptive father took his son with him from job-to-job and through four marriages. They lived in trailers and modest apartments. As Dave Thomas writes in his book, *Well Done,* "It wasn't an easy life by any means, but I survived."[1]

At the tender age of twelve, Dave began working in the restaurant business in Knoxville, Tennessee. The owners of the restaurant, who were immigrants to this country, became his mentors and taught him a very important lesson: if a person tries, he or she can become anything they want to be. This lesson on life became ingrained in Dave's very being.

During the next move, his father took them to Fort Wayne, Indiana. Again, Dave worked for a restaurant. Long hours in the food business led him to drop out of high school at age fifteen. By that time, his relationship with his father had deteriorated and Dave chose to leave his family and take up residence at the YMCA. When Dave turned 18-years old, he enlisted in the Army. After a tour in Germany, he got out of the service, went back to Fort Wayne, and began working at the restaurant where he had worked before. There, he met his wife Lorraine.

He also met Colonel Harland Sanders who was franchising his Kentucky Fried Chicken restaurants. In 1962, Dave and Lorraine moved to Columbus, Ohio, to turn around four failing KFC restaurants. He did it and became an on-paper millionaire, sold his interest and built a backyard swimming pool in the shape of a chicken! The year was 1969 and Dave was only in his thirties. With a love for hamburgers and not ready to retire, Dave created Wendy's. Today, Wendy's International is a multi-billion dollar global company.

Experiencing the success of Wendy's during his lifetime, Dave could have easily kicked back and enjoyed his favorite hobbies of boating and golfing. Yet, this quiet spokesman became a tremendous force in the adoption world. As his widow, Lorraine Thomas, related to me on the phone in May of 2004, "By the time he made the decision to talk about adoption, he had to!"

His own words from *Well Done* bring life to Lorraine's statement:
I wasn't always so front-and-center about being adopted. I would kind of let it trickle out at Wendy's management meetings that I was adopted. These talks mostly centered on the theme "If I Can Make It You Can Too," but sometimes – when I was feeling kind of timid – I'd forget to mention the fact that I was adopted.

One day, a young African-American manager buttonholed me and said, "Dave, when you gave your speech today, you left out the part about being adopted. Why did you do that? I always related to that because I was adopted myself."

That comment hit home for me. After that speech, I always asked two questions in the talks I gave about responsibility in life and doing the right thing. The first was, "How many of you remember the fathers and mothers who gave birth to you?" Nearly everybody raised his or her hand. The second question I asked was, "How many of you never met the father and mother who gave birth to you?" Maybe just one or two in the audience would raise their hand along with me. I was "out of the closet" and proud to be. Doesn't everybody deserve that chance?[2]

I believe the answer is yes. Dave Thomas then took that thought and raised it to an even higher level. "Every child deserves a loving and permanent home." Which brings us to 1990 when President George Bush asked Dave Thomas to be the spokesperson on the adoption initiative, "Adoption Works...For Everyone." Mr. Thomas took on the challenge with enthusiasm and began to speak out on adoption. His message reached millions and I was one of the receivers.

It seemed that my world had been opened to new possibilities. Yes, my adoption was always explained in a very loving way by my parents. My mom, especially, shared a compassionate and grateful message on adoption. Yet, we all have a need to identify with someone outside of our family. Dave Thomas became that person for me. Our adoptions were very different yet very real. Our family lives weren't made of fairy-tale ingredients. What family life is? Still, Dave shared a message of gratitude on adoption that inspires me to this day:

"Adoption made it possible for me to get Minnie Sinclair's love and teaching. Adoption gave me my adoptive mother's care and affection in my early years, even if I don't remember it. And although he had different values than I grew up to believe in, my adoptive father tried his best. Had I not been adopted, I could have ended up as a ward of the state or raised in a county orphanage. So the way I see it, adoption turned out to be a big plus for me."[3]

Dave Thomas possessed the ability to take challenge and heartache and turn it into triumph. I knew I didn't want to let Dave down. I, too, had a duty to give back to adoption what it had given me: hope. I knew someday, someway, I must be a voice in adoption. Dave made my challenge clear, "If you have had the blessing of a good home life yourself, then you do owe something back." (p. 205) Those words could not be anymore true.

In 1992, the Dave Thomas Foundation For Adoption was established. The Foundation set into place both Dave's vision and Wendy's commitment to finding families for those precious children-in-waiting across our country. As is stated on their website:

The Foundation serves as an active voice for the more than 150,000 children in North America's public child welfare system who are waiting for permanent homes and loving families. These kids may be older; part of sibling groups who want to be adopted together; from minority cultures; or physically or mentally challenged. Regardless – they all deserve the love and security of a family.[4]

These children have a much more difficult time realizing their dreams of homes and families. But Dave believed, as do many others who work hard to make these dreams realities, that no child is "unadoptable."

Through the years, I've watched as Dave's Foundation has expanded positive public awareness of adoption, launched groundbreaking research measuring adoption attitudes in the United States, co-hosted one-hour television specials during the holidays that feature successful adoption stories, and has encouraged and educated the public on how to adopt. Perhaps most importantly, I've watched a man dedicate his life to adoption. In 1996-1997, Dave testified before Congress and urged the enactment of an adoption tax credit that would make adoption more affordable. The tax credit, which today stands at $10,160, was signed into law.

Dave passed away during the month of my birth – January. The year was 2002 and I can remember feeling a great sense of loss for a man I never met, but felt as if I had always known. On his passing, he was hailed as the "patron saint of adoption." Dave opened up adoption to the world and, through his example, he opened up my world to the possibilities of giving back to children.

The first time I stepped into the offices of the Dave Thomas Foundation For Adoption I was overwhelmed with a sense of his presence. I was there to meet Rita Soronen, Executive Director of the Foundation. I introduced myself as the Founder of The AML Foundation (Adoption Means Love) and of Adoption Tribe Publishing. During that first meeting in Ohio, Ms. Soronen said, "Dave put an everyman face on adoption." We both appreciated how that was part of the power in his message.

During our second meeting, in May of 2004, Ms. Soronen introduced me to Dave's long-time friend, Ron Musick. Here are Ron's special thoughts on Dave's life:

"I first met Dave in 1966. He was a real character and a practical joker. At first, he didn't speak about being adopted but as the years passed, he began talking about adoption everywhere he went. I saw my dear friend dedicate his life to adoption. He had a big heart for children with special needs and knew the importance of these kids finding permanent and loving homes. As with Wendy's, Dave knew how to make things happen and so when he started the Dave Thomas Foundation For Adoption I knew the lives of children were about to change for the better. He believed in helping one child at a time and his essence was pure. His spirit was all about the children."

That same day, I spoke with Lorraine and she added these thoughts:

"My husband believed in integrity and doing things right. He believed children make a difference."

I am forever grateful for my time with both Lorraine Thomas and Ron Musick. I felt, in a way, I was spending time with Dave during those moments. It was a profound experience and a stirring lesson on Dave's life.

The AML Foundation commits itself to the message of Moving to MUST. We believe Dave Thomas would support this message. It is the promise of AML, in honor of Dave's legacy, to inspire people around the globe to say, "I must adopt a child. "

—Michelle Madrid-Branch, New Mexico

¹Thomas, Dave, with Ron Beyma, *Well Done! The Common Guys Guide to Everyday Success* (New York: Harper Paperbacks, 1995), 8.
²Ibid, 12-13
³Thomas, Dave, *Dave's Way: A New Approach to Old-Fashioned Success* (New York: Berkley Books, 1991), 205-206.
⁴The quotation on the Dave Thomas Foundation For Adoption comes from its website at: www.davethomasfoundationforadoption.org

"My husband believed in integrity and doing things right.
He believed children make a difference."
—Lorraine Thomas

Commitment

We were committed to the adoption process and our resolve was put to the test!

This is a true adoption story filled with what many of our friends call a comedy of errors. Our baby was waiting for us in Florida; unfortunately, so was a tornado. In fact, the tornado touched down in the Sunshine State only ten minutes before we were to land. So our plane was forced to circle the airport until conditions were safe.

Whew! After we finally arrived at the airport, we (me, my husband, and our five-year old daughter) realized that our baggage, along with a car seat, did not make it. Sorting out that situation (which still left us without baggage) took time, enough time to make us two hours late for our arrival at the adoption agency. When we did arrive, our five-year old daughter, whom we hoped would be ecstatic to meet a new baby sibling, was having a meltdown accompanied by screaming and kicking. I thought to myself: "Who in their right mind would hand a baby over to us now?"

Moments later we were taken into a room where, in a little seat, was our little boy, sleeping. He was so tiny. No words can express the emotion I felt. An agency worker placed him in my arms and he immediately felt like my son. We signed the required papers and were told, "Take your baby, he's yours forever."

I was on cloud nine and in somewhat of a daze when we left the agency and headed to our motel. Coming out of my daze, I began noticing the destruction left behind by the tornado. Trees were snapped like toothpicks, and twisted metal from street signs littered the road. We pulled into the motel parking lot, met the front desk attendant, and were promptly told there was no electricity and no phone service.

We couldn't stay with our new baby in a room without electricity, so we began to search for other lodging. After driving for about an hour, we noticed lights! Kmart was open! We went in and began scooping up diapers, bottles, nipples, formula, clothes, powder, and other baby essentials. Remember, we had no baggage so everything we packed for our journey was still missing in action!

The Kmart security guard became suspicious of this odd looking crew, but after hearing our story, we think he believed us!

This leg of our journey came to an end when we located a motel with electricity. Settling in, we then realized that the antibiotics given to us for our baby's eye infection, had been left at the adoption agency.

Here's a quick timeline of the hours that followed:

9:00 pm:	My husband drives back to the agency for the antibiotics.
10:30 pm:	He arrives back with the medication, and food from Wendy's.
11:00 pm:	Realizing we have no can opener for baby formula, we head to a noisy bar, next to the motel, and borrow one.
1:00 am:	I panic as our baby boy is lethargic. I contact our pediatrician and I'm told the medication is likely making him drowsy.
3:00 am:	Our baby finally awakens with a serious hunger. There is no sleep for the rest of the night.

Here's where the fun really begins!

The next morning, our baby receives a clean bill of health from a local doctor. My husband discovers he has lost the keys to our rental car and so our adoption counselor gives us a lift to the airport for replacement keys. En route, we were involved in a three-car collision. Our necks snapped, but the children were safe in their rented car seats.

Getting back to the agency, via police car, we were met by the secretary with car keys in hand. It seems our lost keys were on the counter at the adoption agency the whole time!

We were committed to the adoption process and our resolve was put to the test!

Our adoption story happened many years ago, yet it still feels fresh and vivid. It came with a few bumps in the road, but it is a testament to our commitment in adopting our little boy. We had made the 'move to must' and nothing was going to stop us – not even a tornado!

Our son is a healthy, intelligent, witty, energetic, athletic, and sensitive eleven-year old boy. The first moments of his adoption journey may not be described as 'smooth sailing', but it was worth every emotion. We loved him the second we first looked at him and our love for him is forever.

—*Brenda Caron,* Vermont

Leap of Faith
Katya & Lena

You may wonder why two adults, after having raised three children, wanted to adopt two adolescent girls from Russia. After all, most people our age are ready to divest themselves of possessions and anxieties. So, you can understand why our relatives, friends, acquaintances, and even the judge in Russia were curious as to our motives.

My only answer for their curiosity is that we wanted to be there for two sisters who needed a home, and who needed a bit of hope, as well.

I had retired from teaching high school after thirty-nine years. I had then started a non-profit corporation, providing scholarship funds for needy Russian students who wished to attend Russian universities.

During a visit to the region of Karelia, which is located by the northern border of Finland, I came in contact with a young woman who had been in the Peace Corps in Petrozavodsk, the capital of Karelia. Angie, who was 26-years old and single, had adopted two sisters from the orphanage where she had worked. Angie viewed the adoptions as "the natural thing to do."

My wife and I became interested in the girls still left behind in that orphanage and came to an agreement that we should adopt a couple of those orphaned children. We had the time and the energy and possessed the resources to provide a good home for them.

So, we fought bureaucracies in two countries and made two trips to Russia in the coldest and darkest times of winter. Now we have two daughters and as a friend recently said, "This is where the adventure really begins."

Katya and Lena have been in our lives for just over two months and already, there are many stories and small interactions that are binding us together as a family. Moments from the first two days I remember the best. Here they are.

We met the girls on a Monday, accompanied by our agency's facilitator, a translator, and the director of the orphanage. Katya and Lena were desperate to be adopted and it showed in everything they did or said. The girls were dressed in their best clothes and were trying to be perfect in every way. We, on the other hand, were also trying to be seen as understanding and interested potential parents.

We gave each girl gifts and they shared their photo albums and schoolwork with us. These were important moments, yet, I couldn't get past the feeling that we were all on a blind date of sorts, and nothing seemed quite real.

Reality began for us when we were able to speak with the girls' primary caregiver, Galina, who had known Katya and Lena for ten years. Galina was extremely perceptive and informative as she shared her impressions of the girls. I realized her fondness for them as she wept steadily, showing her mixed emotions about their leaving.

The next afternoon, the girls were scheduled to meet us after school. As we trudged across the snow-packed field leading to the orphanage, I looked up and saw the girls sprinting to greet us. They were very eager to see us again and to be reassured that this adoption process was going to continue.

After that enthusiastic run across a snowy field, there was no doubt that we would stay the course. And so we are. The girls are now here in America with us and are learning English, while slowly adapting to our culture. I remain confident that, despite any barriers and challenges, both girls will succeed in reaching their goals. Katya and Lena are empowered to change their lives. Ultimately, we know the choices leading to those changes will be their choices.

My wife and I are honored to have both girls in our lives. We are all heading toward the future with the same kind of enthusiasm that was displayed on a frozen Russian field when our daughters came leaping into our lives with incredible faith.

—*Don Gould,* Massachusetts

A Kinship Victory/Keeping a Family Together

Stephen & Brandon

My husband, Dale, and I began our adoption journey almost five years ago. Two of our grandchildren had been taken into foster care and their parents' rights were about to be terminated.* Since the state of Maine does not recognize open adoption*, we knew we had to intervene, as the children would soon be available for adoption. We also knew that we might lose them forever, especially if our grandchildren were to be adopted by parents who didn't want us to have contact with them. Our sense of urgency grew and we knew we must act.

The children's caseworker came to our home to meet us and to ask loads of questions. One of those questions was "Have you considered becoming licensed foster parents?" We said, "No, we just want the children to come live with us. We don't see why we have to be their foster parents. We are kin."

The question would not go away, however, so we began to explore the idea of becoming licensed foster parents. To become licensed would require the completion of a home study.* We chose a special young woman whom we knew from KidsPeace International, to conduct the study, which she agreed to do. Because of our relationship, we felt the process would be a little less intrusive with her guidance.

The mindset of "the apple doesn't fall far from the tree," seems to prevail in the state of Maine. We now faced that mindset as it pertained to our grandchildren. There wasn't a stone unturned as we endured two psychological evaluations. Talk about living in a "fish bowl" and "letting it all hang out!" Having successfully passed our evaluations, we soon became licensed therapeutic foster parents.

At the three year point, our grandson, Stephen, was moved into our home and we became his foster parents. He was seven-years old at the time and hooked to his Grampy's hip! Stephen and his Grampy share a very special sport; they love to fish! Cast and reel, cast and reel, cast and reel! On November 13, 2001, our grandson, Stephen, became our son as his adoption was finalized. In his heart, I think he had been our son long before the adoption, calling us mom and dad came naturally from very early on.

In August, Stephen's brother Brandon moved in with us as we officially became his foster parents. The day of his move was also his eleventh birthday. A tremendous celebration took place on this wonderful and long awaited day. Brandon and I have become very close. The one thing we both enjoy is cuddling at night as we watch television. The most memorable nights are when he includes his Panda bear, 'Pandy', in the snuggling. 'Pandy' is very special to Brandon, and when his special bear is allowed to be part of our lives we realize he has begun to trust us and to settle in.

On one very special Thursday, Brandon's caseworker came to see Brandon and announce that she was transferring him into the adoption unit. When she asked Brandon what he thought about it, he replied, "Well it's been a long time coming! I'm happy with it."

Our new family is so grateful for all the help we have received along the way. It has been hard to understand why we had to go through tough times, yet, we remain thankful to everyone who stood by us and supported us through it all. The outcome is a remarkably joyous time in our lives. Brandon and Stephen are living together again after being separated for five years! Dale and I feel as if we have a new lease on life and we're thankful we were moved to say, "We must adopt our grandchildren!" They sure keep us young at heart! P.S. Brandon's adoption is now finalized and his name is DJ — Dale Joseph Martin, Jr.

—*Brenda Martin,* Maine
*Definitions of Termination of Parental Rights (TPR), Open Adoption, and Home Study can be found in the Glossary of Terms.

Thoughts from a Princess

Jennifer

Hello, my name is Jennifer Farrell, Miss New Jersey 2003-2004. I was adopted at birth and have dedicated my year of service as Miss New Jersey to educating the public about adoption and all of its benefits. It is my honor to be able to share my adoption story with you and share in the celebration of such a life changing act of love.

August 22, 1984. . .my birthday. Two days later, I was adopted privately from Maryland. Just like many couples, when my parents got married they dreamed of the day that they would start their family. Sadly, they were unable to conceive so they entered their names into adoption agencies. This was a depressing time for them because there were hardly any babies available for adoption; women were either choosing the road of abortion or single parenting. Finally, after eight years of waiting, my parents received a phone call from a doctor in Maryland (now my godfather) telling them that a baby girl was born and asked them if they would be interested in adopting her. Elated, they drove down to Maryland and picked her up. That little baby was me. My parents had finally gotten their wish and were able to adopt. They continued to keep their name on lists in adoption agencies just in case they could be lucky enough to adopt a second child. They knew their chances were extremely slim, but they never gave up hope. My parents turned this negativity into positive energy and four years later, they adopted my brother from Lutheran Social Services in Trenton, New Jersey.

Being told that I was adopted had always been a part of my life growing up. Ever since I can remember, my mother had explained to me about adoption and how special it was to be adopted. My mother used a very special way to tell me about my adoption by making me a book. This book was a photo album with captions under each picture using very juvenile language. For example, the first page was a picture of my parents on their wedding day. Underneath the picture read, "Mommy and Daddy are getting married. . .one day they want to have a baby." The next picture was one of my aunt, uncle and three young cousins. Others included other family members and their children. However, on the second to last page there was no picture on it. Every time I read that book I always asked why this page was not like the rest. The caption expressed my parents' grief and sadness over not being able to have children. But the book ended on a joyous note. The last page was a picture of myself on the day I was born (not my most photogenic moment by the way) with a caption reading "God's gift to Mommy and Daddy, Jennifer Lynn."

I have found that this book has been such a useful learning tool not only growing up, but to show other children and adults as well.

As Miss New Jersey, I have been able to share the positive message of adoption throughout my state and the surrounding area. Each girl that competes in a pageant, whether it's on a local, state, or national level, must have a plat-form: an issue that the young woman feels strongly about and would like to work on during her year of service. I chose adoption because it is an issue of great concern for millions of Americans, but I feel that there is not enough edu-cation about adoption in our schools or pregnancy counseling centers. I have incorporated my personal experiences as an adopted child and joined forces with many organizations such as the National Council For Adoption and the Children First Foundation to help spread the benefits of adoption.

Being Miss New Jersey allows me to make many different appearances and speak to many different audiences and age groups. As I was speaking in an elementary school on one of my appearances, I asked the second grade children if they knew what adoption meant. A little girl raised her hand and replied, "Sure, Miss New Jersey. . .adoption is when your mom doesn't want you so she gives you to someone that does." That answer from a second grader has helped to motivate me to spread my message and dispel the myths and misconcep-tions that go along with adoption. All of my school speeches have been very positive. When I speak to younger children I keep the lesson very basic and ask the audience if anyone is adopted and I raise my hand with them to make them feel more comfortable. It is such a joy seeing the children's reactions. . .some-times I hear comments like "Look! The princess is adopted too!"
I am so grateful for the opportunity to make a difference in the lives of children by sharing my personal experience and helping to educate these children at a young age so that they can help abolish the prejudices of adoption.

I also feel that my age gives me an advantage when speaking at high schools to young men and women. Being nineteen years old, I am at the opti-mum age of the audience I would like to target most. This is the age where most sexual activity and unplanned pregnancies occur; therefore, the education of adoption is strongly needed. Using my personal experiences as an adopted child and being the same age as my target audience has enabled me to better relate to them and help them absorb my message.

Another tool that has helped to bolster my message is my adoption specialist certification. Last August, I had the opportunity to travel to Orlando, Florida, for a specialist training workshop given by the National Council For Adoption called the Infant Adoption Awareness Training Program. This three-day course consisted of learning ways to speak about adoption in the correct form, how to counsel pregnant women in crisis, and how to adapt the message of adoption depending on the audience that you wish to educate. Having my adoption specialist certification has enabled me to learn the correct terminology and ways to speak about adoption so that the proper message is delivered.

A little boy once told an adoption agency, "The only thing wrong with adoption is what everyone thinks about it." Being an adopted child, I have felt nothing but love from both sides. I feel love from my birthmother, even though I do not know her and have never had any contact with her. I know, however, that she made such an unbelievable sacrifice and chose to put the needs of her child before those of herself. I also feel love from my adoptive parents because they wanted a child more than anything in the world and adopted me with hearts filled with nothing but unconditional love and care. I am so thankful to my birthmother for giving me a second chance at life. This gift of life is the most important and cherished gift one could ever receive.

—*Jennifer Farrell,* Miss New Jersey 2003-2004

Jennifer Farrell, Miss New Jersey
2003-2004

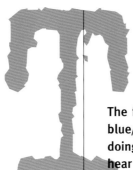

Pasture Prayer
(Dakota's Story)

Dakota

The full moon covered everything with a beautiful blue/gray blanket of light. I was alone in our pasture doing a night check on the horses and all I could hear was the wind chattering through the pines that surrounded our riding ring and small barn. It was hard to concentrate on much of anything that night. We had received a call earlier that week letting us know that a little boy had been born in Savannah and, as long as the birthmother didn't change her mind, he would be our son. It seemed we had been waiting for that call all our lives.

As I stood there quietly, I thought about all that we had been through in the last few years. I thought about our home. A home that had previously been filled with smiles and laughter had become relatively silent due to the multiple infertility treatments we had subjected ourselves to. It had worn us down and had turned us into people we barely recognized. We couldn't go out to eat for fear of running into happy parents with their happy children. We didn't want to see the Hallmark card versions of lives we couldn't have. We had stopped seeing friends. We had stopped seeing family. In essence, we had stopped living.

And then that call had come. It had been like a bright beam of light shining into our thick, suffocating darkness. Could this be the child that we had wanted all these years? Could this be our chance at being a whole family? We were thrilled. But we were also terrified that something would happen to take this potential happiness away from us.

So, with a heavy but hopeful heart, I got on my knees and started praying. I was no stranger to prayer. I had prayed pretty much every day since I was a kid but this prayer was different. It was desperate. This prayer came from a point deep inside me. In a place that I didn't want to admit existed;

the place that ached to be a Dad. The prayer came in shudders and sobs. As I let it pour out of me, I could hear our horses walking quietly to my right side. They came to within ten yards or so and stopped. I could hear their curious breathing in the summer night's air. They kicked up tiny clouds of dust as they quietly pawed at our parched grassless pasture.

"God," I prayed out loud. "I know I could be a great dad if I only had a chance. I'm begging for that chance. Please let me be that little boy's father. I will love him and always be there for him. He will always know he is loved and cherished. He will be surrounded by gentleness and caring for as long as I live. Please, Heavenly Father, just give me a chance. I know I'm not perfect but I do know that I want to be his dad. I'm ready to be his dad. Please, let him come home to us. We've been crushed at the prospect of not having children. The cruelness of that weighs upon us in every waking moment. And now, we have a shot at giving love to a child. Please, God, bring that little boy to us. Our broken hearts need him so badly."

I paused for a moment and ended my prayer. "Thank you, God. Thank you so much."

I stayed on my knees for what seemed like a long time. The tears streaked down my dusty cheeks and were soaked up by the thirsty earth beneath me. Finally, I stood up, gave the horses a pat and looked toward our house with its warm glow in the distance. The prayer had left me exhausted but cleansed. As I walked to the house that summer night, something seemed different. I felt, for the first time in my life, that I was definitely going to be a Dad.

One week later, my pasture prayer was answered. We brought Dakota home.

—Jim Spruell, Georgia

Author's Note: Jim Spruell is a powerful songwriter and musician. He is also a passionate advocate of adoption. I thank him for sharing his ardent and pure emotion that moved him to cry out to the heavens, "I must adopt this boy." *—MMB*

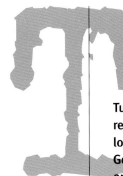

A Brother's Gift
(Savannah's Story)

Tulsa, Oklahoma seemed a million miles away. In reality, it was just three straight days of driving as long as we averaged 75 miles per hour through Georgia, Tennessee, and Arkansas. I figured that, once I hit Oklahoma, I could coast in doing a healthy 65 mph. We hit the road with a fairly new car, a bunch of baby gear loaded in the back, and about a hundred detailed maps.

Gloria, Dakota, and I were headed to Tulsa to meet our newest family member. A little girl named Savannah was about to be brought into the world and we wanted to be there as early on as we could. Some of our friends questioned the idea of bringing Dakota along since he was only four years old but we thought it would help him understand a little of the process we went through when we adopted him. Plus, we couldn't stand the idea of not having him around for the three weeks it would take to get Savannah, and bring her home.

Secretly, I worried about the toll the trip would take on Dakota. On the way to Tulsa, he'd be spending countless hours in the car interrupted only by nights in strange hotel rooms. While in Tulsa, we were going to stay in a corporate apartment that we had found on the Internet. I worried it would be tough on a gentle four-year-old.

As night fell on the third day of driving, I began to have a new worry. How would he feel sharing the spotlight with a new baby sister? How would he react to my wife and I when he saw us devoting much of our time to Savannah? I stared through the windshield and watched my headlights cut into the dark Oklahoma night. I was thankful to finally be in Tulsa but anxious about the weeks ahead. I was especially anxious about Dakota's acceptance of his brand new baby sister.

Savannah was born that Monday. The next morning, we made a quick run to the local drugstore to get film for the camera, more diapers and bottles. As we walked into the store, Dakota ran past us straight to the toy aisle. He rummaged through the toys, moving the items on the shelf forcefully from side to side until he found what he was looking for.

"Look Mom and Dad! Look! This will be a great present for Savannah." Dakota yelled proudly as he presented a squishy baby toy that squeaked when you pressed the middle. "She'll love this." We paid for his gift and left.

Dakota sat quietly in the back seat as we headed to the hospital to finally meet Savannah. He looked out the window and seemed lost in his thoughts. He sat very still and was extremely quiet which was not like him at all. Again, I began to worry about him. Finally, he spoke.

"Mom? Dad? When I give Savannah this present, she'll look at me and say, 'Thanks for the present, big brother. I love you.' Won't that be great?" We smiled and explained that a new baby can't talk yet and, therefore, can't say those things. "I know." He said. "She won't say it with her mouth. She'll say it with her heart."

When we saw Savannah's reaction to her new brother and his hand-picked gift, we knew he was right. She opened her eyes briefly and gave him a soft, gentle smile.

She said it with her heart.

—*Jim Spruell,* Georgia

"Sometimes life's intersections are filled with magic so powerful that you know in that moment that your life is transformed. That magic came in the perfect package of my adopted daughter, Kate. I never needed to give birth. I wanted to parent. And Kate gave me the chance. She has taught, inspired, and challenged me and for that I am ever grateful. and because of her, I decided that I loved parenting so much that she now has two siblings."

—*Dr. Nancy Snyderman,* Medical Correspondent, ABC News

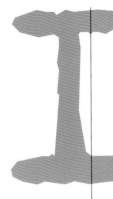

Life is Good
Andrew

I'm thankful to be adopted and I feel blessed!

Every so often, I feel sad that I had to leave my birth mom. Sometimes, it feels like an empty part of your heart that isn't filled with knowing your birth parents. Someday, when I am older, I may get that piece back by trying to find them. But, perhaps when I'm older, I won't want to see them at all.

Right now, I am just trying to live my childhood. I am twelve years old and in the sixth grade. My family helps me do all of the things I love. I play football, hockey, and baseball. I also like skateboarding and snowboarding.

I like my teachers and enjoy my electives like woodworking, pen and ink drawing, cartooning, and the school newspaper. Right now, I am writing an article on the TV programs kids like to watch! In my school cafeteria, I can choose the food I want to eat each day and the cooks make the food just like I ask.

I like being grateful. I am grateful to the social workers that helped place me with my family.

My life is good because of adoption. I have great parents and a cool sister. I am taken care of by my family in a super way, and I never want that to change.

—*Andrew Burke,* New Hampshire

7.

My Journey to Healing the Heart

Gratitude is essential in life. Living in a state of gratitude is key. We must understand consequence and its place in life. Understanding that every choice has an impact on not just the individual making the choice, but on all others who are affected by that particular decision.

Even a child – an innocent life! Presenting the truth to a child regarding choices that were made, for him or her, is a tremendous gift even if the truth brings feelings of pain and hurt. Truth must be known.

For me, as a person of adoption, forgiveness came on an evening in Britain when Jim unveiled his soul to me, along with the personal pain he'd carried with him for so long. Jim is the husband of my birth-mother. He is not my birthfather, but his decision was one of the most powerful forces that separated this child from her birth-mum. Jim was in the Royal Air Force, away on duty, when he learned that my mum, his wife, was six months pregnant with another man's child.

Years later, when I was in my teens, Jim and I sat down together at a small village pub in England.

"Before you were born, I met your birthfather and tried to sort out what should be done," Jim said to me with his hands cupped together. He looked at me and added, "He didn't want to be a father – he was single and liked it that way." There was a fairly long pause.

"I felt anger at the good-looking son-of-a-_____," he emphasized. Jim and I shared an uncomfortable laugh. Then, his steely blue eyes began to tear, "I said to him, if you won't be the father then I shall have to make the decision on what happens to this child."

Jim's voice dropped to an emotional whisper. "When you were born, you looked just like him. When I looked at you, it was like looking at him. What was I to do?" Jim looked at me through flowing tears. "I made the decision which I thought was right, but darling, the second we let you go, I lost my soul, and I haven't found it since."

"Perhaps I can help you retrieve your soul," I said. "You see, Jim, I am okay and I have been loved by a family that I cannot imagine my life without. My parents love me and I love them. I have two brothers whom I adore. Yes, I was innocent in the decisions – the choices, that surrounded my early life – but I refuse to be angry over them and I refuse to be angry at those who made the decisions." I touched his hand. "I forgive you, Jim, and I understand your pain – I share your pain, but I am grateful for the life given me and for the family I call my own. There is healing in truth and I thank you for sharing yours." I then added, "Please let go of the guilt and take back your soul because I am okay."

"Thank you," Jim said, "Thank you." It was, at this moment, when I realized the transformation that had finally occurred in my life. I had become the healer because I was no longer in need of healing.

This was my winged migration, as I opened my heart to comfort the man whose decision helped separate this child from her birthmother, so long ago. Together, Jim and I found an inner sense of peace and a place of rest.

Ah, the breeze on that spiritual mountaintop lifted me up as I spread my wings and soared to a higher place of understanding.

Soul to soul – Jim and I were one. We have never spoken of this moment again. Yet, it will remain as one of the most essential junctures in my life.

May all who are touched by adoption find their own sense of peace, of understanding and of triumph! And may they find their own wings of flight to carry them to others in need of healing.

—*Michelle Madrid-Branch,* New Mexico

From Michelle's family album...

My mother poses in Hong Kong

My father, a handsome U.S. Airman, in Hong Kong

My mother in Taiwan where the seeds of adoption were planted

Dave, Michelle, and Mark, our sibling journey begins...

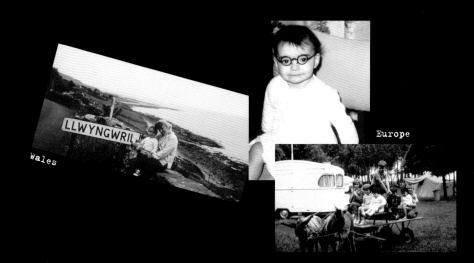

Wales

Europe

Happy, imaginative,
and loved!

Dave, Michelle, and Mark, our sibling journey
continues...

England

Adoring mother

Mom and Dad with me on my wedding day
photo courtesy of Cathy Maier Callahan

Glossary of Terms

Asperger Syndrome: Asperger Syndrome or (Asperger's Disorder) is a neurobiological disorder named for a Viennese physician, Hans Asperger, who in 1944 published a paper which described a pattern of behaviors in several young boys who had normal intelligence and language development, but who also exhibited autistic-like behaviors and marked deficiencies in social and communication skills. Individuals with AS can exhibit a variety of characteristics and the disorder can range from mild to severe. Persons with AS show marked deficiencies in social skills, have difficulties with transitions or changes and prefer sameness. They often have obsessive routines and may be preoccupied with a particular subject of interest. They have a great deal of difficulty reading nonverbal cues (body language) and very often the individual with AS has difficulty determining proper body space. Often overly sensitive to sounds, tastes, smells, and sights, the person with AS may prefer soft clothing, certain foods, and be bothered by sounds or lights no one else seems to hear or see. It's important to remember that the person with AS perceives the world very differently. Therefore, many behaviors that seem odd or unusual are due to those neurological differences and not the result of intentional rudeness or bad behavior, and most certainly not the result of "improper parenting." (O.A.S.I.S. Online Asperger Syndrome Information and Support)

ADHD (Attention Deficit Hyperactivity Disorder):
ADHD is a documented illness that starts in childhood. It can change the way children act, think, and feel. Nearly all children are overactive and inattentive at times, but for ADHD children and their families, their behavior can be extreme and disruptive. ADHD is thought to affect between 3% and 5% of the school age population. In general, ADHD is estimated to be 3 or 4 times more common in boys. For

some, there is remission at puberty but for others the condition, if untreated, continues to blight their adult life. Generally the ADHD child is unable to concentrate, constantly moves around, and has poor school performance compared with intelligence. (AdhdNews.com)

Down Syndrome: Named after John Langdon Down, the first physician to identify the syndrome, Down syndrome is the most frequent genetic cause of mild to moderate mental retardation and associated medical problems and occurs in one out of 800 live births, in all races and economic groups. Down syndrome is a chromosomal disorder caused by an error in cell division that results in the presence of an additional third chromosome 21 or "trisomy 21." (National Institute of Child Health & Human Development)

FAS (Fetal Alcohol Syndrome): Fetal alcohol syndrome (FAS) is a condition characterized by abnormal facial features, growth retardation, and central nervous system problems. It can occur if a woman drinks alcohol during pregnancy. Children with FAS may have physical disabilities and problems with learning, memory, attention, problem solving, and social/behavioral problems. (National Center on Birth Defects and Developmental Disabilities)

Home Study: The laws of every State and the District of Columbia require all prospective adoptive parents (no matter how they intend to adopt) to participate in a home study. This process has three purposes: to educate and prepare the adoptive family for adoption, to gather information about the prospective parents that will help a social worker match the family with a child whose needs they can meet, and to evaluate the fitness of the adoptive family. (National Adoption Information Clearinghouse)

Indian Child Welfare Act: The Indian Child Welfare Act (ICWA) is a federal law, which regulates placement proceedings involving Indian children. If your child is a member of a tribe or eligible for membership in a tribe, your family has the right to protection under the ICWA. These rights apply to any child protective case, adoption, guardianships, termination of parental rights action, runaway/truancy matter, or voluntary placement of your children. The ICWA was created in 1978 by the federal government in order to re-establish tribal authority over the adoption of Native American children. The goal of the act when it passed in 1978 was to strengthen and preserve Native American families and culture. (National Indian Child Welfare Association)

M.A.P.P. (Model Approach to Partnerships in Parenting Program): A 10-week, 30-hour course in foster and adoption training. The course is for those people considering becoming foster care parents (either 'emergency' or long-term foster care) as well as looking to adopt through the foster-care program.

Open Adoption: Open, or fully disclosed adoptions allow adoptive parents, and often the adopted child, to interact directly with birth parents. Open adoption falls at one end of an openness communication continuum that allows family members to interact in ways that feel most comfortable to them. In semi-open or mediated adoptions, information is relayed through a mediator (e.g., an agency caseworker or attorney) rather than through direct contact between the birth and adoptive families. In confidential adoptions, no identifying information is exchanged. (National Adoption Information Clearinghouse)

Parental Rights: Parental rights are a group of rights that includes rights to seek custody and visitation with your child, and the right to make important decisions about education, medical care, money and religion for your child.

Termination of Parental Rights (TPR): When a parent's rights to his/her child are terminated, the parent loses all of the above stated rights and has no grounds to try and get visitation with or custody of the child again. The purpose of terminating a parent's rights is to legally "free" a child to be adopted by someone else.

Josh, Tom and Ana

Tom Morin
Graphic Designer

I design books for a living and I read books for pleasure. I love both. From art books to history books to cookbooks, I have designed, typeset and produced them all.

It was, however, not until Michelle Madrid-Branch asked me to be part of the "Adoption Means Love" team, that I designed a book on this subject; one of which is very close to my heart. Eleven years ago I adopted my daughter, Ana.

I remember flying off to the Dominican Republic to pick up my little girl; 'my little peanut.' Ana was just eleven-days old. Dressed in pink and nestled in my arms, she seemed ready to bring so much excitement and happiness to our world. Ana's brother Josh, met us at Kennedy Airport on our flight back to the States.

Once the formalities and legalities are left behind, you are parents. You have the same responsibilities, goals, and lessons of love to share as any other parent.

We are a family. Josh only knows Ana as his sister. I only know her as my daughter. We are all very lucky!

—TM

I wish to thank Isabella Gonzales, who did all of the typesetting for this book. Isabella and I reside and work in Galisteo, New Mexico with our two black labs, Jessy and Rosie.

Cathy and Bella

Cathy Maier Callanan
Photographer

Cathy Maier Callanan dreamed of adopting a child when she was just a little girl. The dream came true when her daughter, Bella, was placed in her arms. Adopting Bella has forever changed Cathy's world for the better.

"Bella teaches me so much each day and I cannot imagine life without my beautiful daughter."

Cathy commits her heart daily to a powerful vision: a world where all children have loving homes. She knows this vision can be realized through individuals taking action, trusting their hearts, and bringing that special child into their lives through adoption.

Cathy is respected nationally for her creative and innovative approach to wedding and portrait photography. Her images are featured in national magazines including *Town & Country, Bride's* (a Conde Naste publication) *B for Savvy Brides, Camera Arts, Studio Photography* and *Design, Rangefinder, and Popular Photography.* In addition, she is co-founder and co-owner of the internationally renowned Santa Fe Photography and Digital Workshops.

—CMC

Thanks to Sarah Bishop-Root, my assistant for her dedication to this project and her support in gathering the images.

© Cathy Maier Callanan

Michelle Madrid-Branch
Author

We recommend the
following websites for
further adoption
information:
**National Council For
Adoption**
www.adoptioncouncil.org

**National Adoption
Information Clearinghouse**
http://naic.acf.hhs.gov

**Dave Thomas Foundation
For Adoption**
www.davethomasfoundation
foradoption.org

A portion of proceeds
from the sale of this
book support
**The AML Foundation
(Adoption Means Love)**

Michelle Madrid-Branch is Founder of ***Adoption Tribe Publishing*** and ***The AML Foundation (Adoption Means Love).***

As a person of adoption and a former Emmy-Nominated television news journalist, Michelle is focusing her writing talents on adoption awareness and pride. With endless enthusiasm, she works to create a world where adoption is celebrated on every continent and all adoptable children have permanent families to call their own.

Michelle Madrid-Branch is a recipient of the 2004 Congressional Angels in Adoption Award. She is author of the children's book, ***The Tummy Mummy,*** which has been heralded for its poignant and tender message of adoption love. Michelle resides in Santa Fe, New Mexico and is a proud wife and mother.

www.adoptionmeanslove.org

Creating a wave of adoption pride, understanding and awareness around the globe.©